WHY WAR?

ESSAYS AND ADDRESSES
ON WAR AND PEACE

Why War?

ESSAYS AND ADDRESSES
ON WAR AND PEACE

BY

NICHOLAS MURRAY BUTLER

President of Columbia University
President of the American Academy of Arts and Letters
President of the Carnegie Endowment for International Peace
Membre de l'Institut de France

KENNIKAT PRESS, INC./PORT WASHINGTON, N. Y.

WHY WAR?

ESSAY AND GENERAL LITERATURE INDEX REPRINT SERIES

TO THE YOUTH OF AMERICA

WHOSE PRIVILEGE AND DUTY IT WILL BE

TO TAKE THE LEAD IN BRINGING ABOUT

A WORLD-WIDE ORGANIZATION OF NATIONS

FOR THE ESTABLISHMENT AND PROTECTION

OF PROSPERITY AND PEACE

CONTENTS

INTRODUCTION

These essays and addresses are appeals to public opinion which have been made during the years 1938 and 1939 on either side of the Atlantic. Their object is two-fold: first, to convince the leaders of public opinion that the only sure way to prevent war is for the nations of the world to unite to remove the causes of war; and, second, that, violent hostilities having broken out on three continents, the minds of men must now be turned to such post-war settlement of those differences which have brought about hostilities as will pave the way to an orderly and peaceful world. These two aims and courses of action have been emphasized in differing language and from various points of view, but they have dominated and guided each and every one of these appeals.

Persistent emphasis on a purely emotional attitude toward war and peace is one of the gravest obstacles to work for the establishment of peace. Those who take this attitude appear to think that nothing more is necessary. The mere holding of mass meetings, the passing of resolutions denouncing war and the making of public demonstrations against war, highly emotional in character, serve no practical purpose whatsoever. Nowhere in the world could a public demonstration in favor of war as such be organized by anybody. Yet wars exist.

When war, whether declared or undeclared, is begun,

it is because of the fact that populations almost unanimously in favor of peace have not yet been able so to control their governments as to force those governments to meet international differences without armed conflict. The peoples of the world are opposed to war. The pressing problem is that they shall so control their several governments as to require these governments to take united action to remove the causes of war.

NICHOLAS MURRAY BUTLER

COLUMBIA UNIVERSITY
IN THE CITY OF NEW YORK
February 12, 1940

I

WHY WAR?

An address at the celebration of Peace Day
under the auspices of the
International Business Machines Corporation
at the New York World's Fair,
May 4, 1939

WHY WAR?

Why war? In this year of grace, 1939 of the Christian era, why is the whole world at war, economic war, emotional war, intellectual war, and shivering under the threat of military war?

How can such a condition be possible? After all that has been said and done through centuries of growing and ripening civilization to raise mankind, wherever he may be, to a higher level of satisfaction and accomplishment and to bring him into relations with his fellow men that will supply new sources of comfort and satisfaction as his years of life pass on, how is this present outlook possible? What has happened?

Bluntly, there has been, and there is, a complete breakdown of moral conviction and moral principles in respect to national and international policies and relations, and an appalling incapacity on the part of the citizens of the world's few free governments that are left to rise to the heights of their responsibility and opportunity.

If you will take the written public record, war is impossible. Every civilized nation has formally and openly renounced it as an instrument of national policy. Why, then, has it not been renounced? Bluntly, again, because governments have not kept their word and have demonstrated that they can no longer be trusted to keep their word.

In consequence, every nation, east and west, north and south, is pouring all its resources, and far more than its available resources, into expenditure for what it calls defense. No government under any circumstance is preparing for offense. Every government is preparing for defense. If that be true, why is preparation for defense necessary? Because no one believes the protestations of governments.

We are living in an age where the ordinary relationships of nations no longer exist. The forms and rules and laws which have been developing for two hundred or three hundred years and which we thought had established themselves in an elaborate and highly useful code of international law and conduct have all been thrown to the winds, and we are now confronted by pressure politics in the international field of a sort with which we are quite familiar on a much smaller scale in the national field.

This plan of pressure politics aims to achieve revolutionary results without war by threatening war, and the practical question is, where will the line be found when that threat of war will find itself tempted to cause and to undertake actual military operations?

One of the outstanding statesmen of Europe said to me in private conversation a few months ago that the appalling thing was that all this trouble in the world is being caused by not to exceed twelve hundred or fifteen hundred men. He insisted that the peoples everywhere in these democracies, in these totalitarian states, in Asia and South America, want peace and prosperity, but that some twelve or fifteen hundred human beings in positions of great responsibility and authority, that authority being largely based on emotional grounds, held the policies of the world today in their hands.

What can be done about it? There is only one answer, and that is that these peoples themselves must either compel their existing governments to do as they wish, or they must find new instruments of government that will respond to their peaceful ideals and cease these policies of pressure and force and threat which are not only terrifying the whole world, but are making impossible any return to prosperity and happiness until these heavy clouds are removed.

Think what must be the feeling of the mothers of the world as they look out on this scene. Many of them remember only too well what happened to their husbands and their sons twenty-five years ago. How many of them can face with equanimity what might, within twenty-four hours, begin to happen to the husbands and sons of today? What is the use of trade, what is the use of industry, what is the use of commerce, what is the use of effort, what is the use of trying to gain some return from all these in order to make mankind more comfortable, more fortunate and better protected in old age and adversity? What is the use of it all? We are pouring out not only the world's earnings, but the world's savings, savings for a thousand years, and those savings are not illimitable. There comes a time when they will have gone, and what will the world do then unless it desists from this policy of threats and this rule of force and terror? What will happen?

In the last war, there was destroyed a value equal to that of five countries like France plus five countries like Belgium. Should there be another war tomorrow, that destruction might be of the value of five countries like Great Britain, or five countries like the United States of

America. And what would history have to say of that
one hundred or two hundred years from today, as a comment upon our intelligence, our courage and our capacity
to maintain civilization on the high plane—what?

Believe me, there is need for leadership, a new kind
of leadership; not the leadership which meets force with
force, not the leadership which regards war as inevitable
and spends time and countless money in preparing for
it, but leadership that understands that there is only one
way to get rid of war, and that is to remove the causes
of war, and that to remove the causes of war means international co-operation and international effort on an economic, a monetary, a social and a political scale.

Why should not the government of the United States
go back to its traditional leadership in this field which it
had in its hand from 1899 until 1919 and which it has
let pass away? Why should we not go back with our vast
population, our high ideals, our wide political experience, our economic power, our convinced belief in peace
and its possibility? Why should we not go back and
make the reply on the behalf of the government which
President McKinley made to the great rescript of the
Czar of all the Russias, one of the greatest documents
in human history, when in 1898 he asked the nations of
the world to do just what I am proposing they return to
do now? Why should we not go back to President Mc-
Kinley's great statement made with superb eloquence on
the day before the assassin took his life: "The period of
exclusiveness is past"? Why should we not go back to
Secretary Elihu Root's instructions to the American delegation to the second Hague Conference in 1908 which
resulted in arranging for a Permanent Court of International Justice? Why should we not go back to the

famous Joint Resolution passed by the Congress of the United States on June 24, 1910, by unanimous vote in each House, calling upon the President of the United States to lead in the organization of the nations of the world for peace with international security protected by the combined navies of the world?

Twenty-nine years ago the Congress of the United States passed that resolution without a dissenting vote in either House. Then came the Great War, the sad results of which I need not repeat. But here we are today faced with this perfectly appalling calamity, and voices are saying that it is no concern of ours, that we need not care if one neighbor murders his neighbor, or if one human being assaults another human being, so long as they do not live in our house or belong to our family. That sort of neutrality is gross immorality.

The sooner and the more completely that it is pronounced as such and denounced as such, the farther shall we be along on the road to peace. That sort of conduct leads inevitably to war, no matter what professions may accompany it. If the United States Government, from its present commanding position, can, for the moment, keep itself outside of and above the particular causes of conflict—except economic, in which we are involved already—that are likely to lead to military war, why should not that Government today say to the whole world, "We remember what we said in 1898 to the Czar of all the Russias. We remember what we said in 1908 which led to the Permanent Court of International Justice. We remember what our Congress voted in 1910 to promote the peace of the world, and today we say to you, there is where we stand and that is what we propose to do."

II

TOWARD A FEDERAL WORLD

An address delivered at the Parrish Art Museum,
Southampton, Long Island,
September 3, 1939

TOWARD A FEDERAL WORLD

This year of grace marks the one hundred and fiftieth anniversary both of the French Revolution and of the organization of the government of the United States under the Federal Constitution. It is therefore an anniversary of commanding importance in the history of man's attempt to arrive at a form of government which shall be both effective and just.

It is not generally realized that the government of these United States, which came formally into existence a century and a half ago, is now the oldest of all the governments existing in the world. It is the only one which has not been changed in essential principles or revolutionized during the past century and a half. This fact is, of itself, a tribute to the wisdom and the foresight of those whom we so gladly call the Founding Fathers. On the continent of Europe every government which has not been wholly made over since the World War came into being in its present form only after the Napoleonic Wars, or, as in the case of France, after the Franco-Prussian War of 1870–71. The government of Great Britain, responding to the pressure of the steadily growing liberal movement during the eighteenth and nineteenth centuries, was substantially changed both as to its center of gravity and as to its governmental procedure following the Reform Bill of 1832, the Parliamentary Representation Act of 1867 and the Parliament Act of 1911. The last-named act gave the relations between the House of Commons and the House of Lords their present form. Still later, in 1931,

the Statute of Westminster, an act of the greatest importance in the history of constitutional government and
public law, brought into existence the British Commonwealth of Nations as now constituted. This act applied
the federal principle to legislatively independent members of a great empire scattered all around the world.
The governments of the Central American and South
American peoples are all younger than the government
of the United States. The governments on the continents of Africa and of Asia have been and still are in a
constant state of flux, and it remains to be seen what
their more permanent form is to be.

When the Federal Constitution had been agreed upon
by the Philadelphia Convention on September 17, 1787,
and submitted to each of the thirteen independent and
sovereign states for their consideration and hoped-for
ratification, Benjamin Franklin, most far-seeing of men,
wrote these words to Monsieur Grand, a friend in
France, under date of October 22, 1787, sending him at
the same time a copy of the proposed new Federal Constitution for the American states:

> If it succeeds, I do not see why you might not in Europe carry
> the project of good Henry the Fourth into execution, by form-
> ing a federal union and one grand republic of all its different
> states and kingdoms, by means of a like convention, for we had
> many interests to reconcile.[1]

It would seem plain, therefore, that those men who
planned with so much wisdom and so much foresight the
Constitution of the United States felt that they were
dealing with forces and ideals which might well be not

[1]*Works of Benjamin Franklin,* edited by John Bigelow (New York:
1888) Volume IX, p. 442.

only American but world-wide. They were the very opposite of isolationists.

Something of the same sort characterized the chief spokesmen of the French Revolution. They, too, believed that they were building not for France alone but for all Europe. The quick outburst of reaction which marked the twenty years of the rule of Napoleon Bonaparte pushed any such hope and ambition far into the background.

As a result of these happenings of one hundred and fifty years ago and their influence, the civilized world seemed far on the way toward becoming a world in which the principles of Democracy ruled and would express themselves either in the form of a democratic monarchy, as in Great Britain, Belgium, the Netherlands and the Scandinavian countries, or in that of a democratic republic, as in the United States, France and Switzerland. In almost every other country of the world, even in Germany and in Russia, there were clear signs that the principles of liberalism were, in one form or another, finding steadily increasing expression and influence.

When the Great War came a quarter-century ago, it was quickly interpreted by the President of the United States as fundamentally a contest between democratic and anti-democratic principles of government. His famous phrase, a war to make the world safe for democracy, was heard in every land and was almost universally accepted as both the explanation and the justification of that stupendous struggle. The contradictory and unhappy result is now so obvious as to need no comment. The passions and ambitions which were set loose by that great war have been operating and still operate to do the principles of democracy greater damage than has ever heretofore been inflicted on them from any source. The story of that war is now written large in history. Every single cause for which the allied nations fought and for which they made such enormous sacrifices, and which on Armistice Day, November 11, 1918, they thought had been finally gained, is now seen to have been lost. On the other hand, every cause for which their opponents contended and which was thought to be lost, is now clearly seen to have been gained. In short, that great war, with all its terrible sacrifice of life, of the comfort and happiness of tens of millions of human beings and of the world's savings for generations, was absolutely futile.

What is the lesson to be learned from all this? Surely it is now the clear demonstration of more than a thousand years of nation-building that the doctrine of national sovereignty is both unsound and dangerous. That doctrine can only lead, as it has led, to the notion that each and every established government is a law unto itself and not subject to any limitations or control in its dealings with other governments. Put bluntly, this means that when two of these so-called sovereign governments cannot agree upon any matter which affects them both, then recourse shall be had to force, which is war. Constituted as they are, human beings in control of the administration of governments that claim to be sovereign will be constantly at war, regardless of the loss of life or of property which must always accompany war, whether successful or unsuccessful.

From a situation such as this there are but two paths of escape. The one is universal world domination by a single government. On a larger or a smaller scale, this end has been sought time and time again for fully three thousand years. Oriental peoples sought it; Alexander the Great sought it; Julius Cæsar and his successors at the head of the Roman Empire sought it. Charlemagne would have been glad to seek it, as would Napoleon Bonaparte a thousand years later. The German Reichsfuehrer of today has it plainly in mind. Surely after all these illuminating experiences it ought to be obvious to every one that the world cannot be unified under a single social, economic and political control. This could not be done when the world was relatively a very simple place, but now that invention and modern science have made it so complicated, as well as so interdependent in its every part, world domination by a single power has become more impossible than ever. The search for world domination or even for domination over a considerable part of the earth's surface means and must mean constant and almost continuous war. Different backgrounds of national history, of language, of social and political experience, to say nothing of climate and of the conditions of life, have made any such form of world unification as the ancient empire builders sought a purely imaginary aim. It has and can have no relation to reality.

If, then, sovereignty be denied to governments of any kind, what is it that in last resort should rule and guide the action of men and shape the public policies of the governments which the several nations may from time to time set up? Obviously, it is the moral law.

This moral law is not difficult to understand. Every one, however great, knows when he is telling the truth, when he is acting in unselfish regard for the welfare of his fellow men and when he is subjugating the gain-seeking or the power-seeking motive to higher and more constructive principles. The practical-minded man will see this. The theoretical person who loves to deal only with words and with the impressions of the moment may take some time, perhaps a long time, to learn it. Unless it be learned, however, there is no escape from that barbarism which is return to the jungle.

The alternative to the hopeless attempt at universal world domination by a single government is that world-wide application of the federal principle which has already played so influential a part in modern political history and which alone has the power to make it possible for modern man to solve in permanent fashion, through the co-operation of nations, his unbelievably difficult and complicated problems—economic, social and political.

The federal principle and its application upon an increasingly large scale have been before the minds of men for hundreds of years. One seer after another and one far-sighted statesman after another have proclaimed and interpreted the federal principle as essential to the peaceful, orderly maintenance and development of civilization. Few declarations of this principle are more significant or more definite than this prophecy written in autograph by Victor Hugo on the wall of the model of the room in which he died in the Place des Vosges, Paris:

I represent a party which does not yet exist: the party of revolution, civilization. This party will make the twentieth century. There will issue from it first the United States of Europe, then the United States of the World.[2]

[2]Bartlett's *Familiar Quotations* (Boston: 1937), p. 1069.

This federal principle must not be confused with group or regional alliances between governments for their own aggrandizement, no matter what may happen to the rest of the world. The federal principle, as supremely manifested in the Federal Constitution of the United States and in the Statute of Westminster which created the British Commonwealth of Nations, makes it not only possible but natural for a Vermont, a South Dakota, an Idaho and a Utah, or for a Newfoundland, a Union of South Africa and a New Zealand to enter a political partnership upon equal terms with a New York, an Illinois and a Texas in the one case, or with a Canada and Australia in the other. Under a properly organized federal system, the population or the wealth of a political partner gives no advantage in all that is essential to citizenship and to political liberty. The influence of the more populous and the richer peoples will always be dominant or nearly so, but that dominance will be exercised under the limitations of the articles of federation. This will involve no injustice and no discrimination against the less populous and the less wealthy members of the federation.

The practical question is, How can this tremendous and crucial problem be lifted from the region of discussion to that of early and definite action? It is plain that the world cannot wait.

One of the lessons which experience teaches is that in large matters of this kind too much must not be attempted at once. The overwhelming majority of men have to be taught, and it takes a long time to teach them. The Federal Government of the United States stands before the whole world as instructor in what the federal principle may accomplish over an enormous area with a huge and varied population. Nevertheless, if the attempt were made to organize the entire world in a satisfactory federation at once, it would probably fail, either wholly or in large part. The differences of background, of inheritance, of experience and of language might be found too great to permit an effective world-wide federal union at one stroke. The path of progress, obviously, is to promote the early organization of a world federation which would include, if not all European and Asiatic peoples, then those which are sufficiently self-controlled and like-minded to make a beginning possible. In due time and after the value of the federal principle had received new illustration, it would become practicable to go a step farther and begin to bring more of the national governments into a still larger union. There is no reason why those states which are called totalitarian should not be included in such a federal union, provided they will cease striving to extend their areas and their control by force, and will accept, honestly and completely, the principles upon which such a federal union is built. We need have no concern with the form of government which any independent people adopts for itself, if only it keeps its word and respects its international and federal obligations.

There is nothing new about this proposal to extend the federal principle. If mankind had shown itself capable of learning by experience, great progress would have been made centuries ago in developing a world system of federal unions which might easily have become a single world-wide union long before this twentieth century. The story of these attempts and of the measure of success which they severally achieved will be found in very succinct form in the little volume entitled *Federations: A Study in Comparative Politics*, written by D. G. Karve, Professor of History and Economics at Fergusson College, Poona, India, and published seven years ago.[3] It will surprise many readers of the present day to learn how clearly this idea of federation was in the minds of men almost from the very beginning of political organization. The Dutch Union between the provinces of the Low Countries, which lasted for more than two centuries, and the Swiss Federation, which is the oldest of all the existing federal states, are particularly rich in opportunity for study. In fact, the Swiss Federation and the United States of America may be regarded as the two most productive research laboratories in which the student and the builder of new federations may best carry on his work.

The history of Switzerland offers abundant material for guidance in dealing with this problem today. That country has many small towns and cities of only moderate size. Its physical formation, with high mountains, deep valleys and many streams, provides almost compelling invitation to the development of many small communities, living largely in isolation and in independent social and political life. Some two thirds of the population speak German and most of the remaining one third speak French, although there is a very considerable number of those whose language is Italian. The population is divided almost equally between Protestants and Catholics, with a greater number of Protestants. These people, so placed and with such diverse back-

[3]Oxford University Press, 1932. 318 pp.

grounds, have been successful, it would appear, in working out a plan for national unity which is wholly consonant with civil liberty and with local self-government. If the people of Switzerland have been able to achieve this great end, why should not others be able to follow their example and go and do likewise? Switzerland, of course, has passed through its difficult periods. These were in part due to religious strife, and in part to the rivalry between urban and rural cantons. But, taken as a whole and looking back over more than five hundred years, it is clear that Switzerland has a most important lesson to teach this modern world.

Had the Republic of Czechoslovakia, at the time of its organization in 1919, been based upon the cantonal system, its history during the past twenty years might have been very different and far happier. A Czechoslovakia composed of, say, five Czech cantons, two Slovak cantons, two German cantons, one Polish canton and one Hungarian canton, following the example of Switzerland, might well have been able to weather the storms which have marked the attempt to give to this splendid people the independent economic and political organization which they desire and should have.

In relation to this vitally important matter we have reached a point where the responsibility of the people of the United States is outstanding and imperative. As economic and political theories have developed and found expression in various governments, whether in Europe or in Asia, it has become impossible, at least for some time to come, for any other government than that of the United States to give the leadership for which the world is waiting. Had our American political acts during the past generation been true to our professions, and had the elected representatives of the two great political parties, when in office at Washington, kept the pledges which those parties had made to the American people in one political campaign after another, this world would today have been far on the way toward successful organization to promote prosperity and to preserve peace.

With the exception of the eight years of Woodrow Wilson's administration, the Republican party was in power at Washington from 1896 to 1932. Beginning with President McKinley's notable statement, "The period of exclusiveness is past," made at Buffalo, September 5, 1901, the Republican party made one declaration after another in favor of definite and progressive policies of international co-operation to prevent war. It would be difficult to find a more definite pledge to the people than this which was contained in the Republican National Platform of 1920:

The Republican party stands for agreement among the nations to preserve the peace of the world. We believe that such an international association must be based upon international justice, and must provide methods which shall maintain the rule of public right by the development of law and the decision of impartial courts, and which shall secure instant and general international conference whenever peace shall be threatened by political action, so that the nations pledged to do and insist upon what is just and fair may exercise their influence and power for the prevention of war.

We believe that all this can be done without the compromise of national independence, without depriving the people of the United States in advance of the right to determine for them-

selves what is just and fair when the occasion arises, and without
involving them as participants and not as peace-makers in a
multitude of quarrels, the merits of which they are unable to
judge.

Even more striking is this extract from a speech delivered by Senator Warren G. Harding at Marion,
Ohio, on August 28, 1920, when a candidate for the
presidency. It is probable that it was this speech which
ensured his election. Here are his words:

> The other type is a society of free nations, or an association of
> free nations, or a league of free nations, animated by consider-
> ations of right and justice, instead of might and self-interest,
> and not merely proclaimed an agency in pursuit of peace, but so
> organized and so participated in as to make the actual attainment
> of peace a reasonable possibility. Such an association I favor with
> all my heart, and I would make no fine distinction as to whom
> credit is due. One need not care what it is called. Let it be an
> association, a society, or a league, or what not, our concern is
> solely with the substance, not the form thereof.

The Republican National Platforms of 1924, 1928
and 1932 contained like declarations, varying somewhat
in language, but essentially one and the same. What
was done by the Republican senators and representatives
to keep those solemn pledges to the American people in
reference to all which concerned their highest interests?

The record of the Democrat party is similar. Quite
apart from the vision and the influence of Woodrow
Wilson, here is the language used by Governor James
M. Cox at Dayton, Ohio, on August 7, 1920, when candidate for the presidency in opposition to Senator Harding:

Organized government has a definite duty all over the world. The house of civilization is to be put in order. The supreme issue of the century is before us and the nation that halts and delays is playing with fire. The finest impulses of humanity, rising above national lines, merely seek to make another horrible war impossible.

Four years later on August 11, 1924, the Democrat candidate for the presidency, John W. Davis, spoke these words at Clarksburg, West Virginia:

We favor the World Court in sincerity. . . . We wish to see America as a nation play her part in that reconstruction of the economic life of Europe which has proven itself so indispensable to our well-being and prosperity.

The Democrat National Platforms of 1928 and of 1932 reflected the same point of view and recorded the same purpose.

Why is it, then, that nothing has been done? What has become of responsible government in a democracy if those great ends which the people have been asked to support, and which they have so earnestly supported, are left to die by parliamentary ineptitude and parliamentary cowardice? What wonder is it that the dictators point with scorn to what they describe as the inefficiency and the uselessness of Democracy! It must be evident that Democracy is only playing into the hands of the dictators when it writes for itself a record such as this. Surely, every public interest of the American people, whether moral, economic or political, calls for their quick leadership in organizing what in President Harding's words may be an association, a society, a league or what not, of nations, to take over the solution of the world's grave and most disturbing problems.

Let me once again call attention to the amazing resolution which passed both Houses of Congress in June, 1910, without a single dissenting vote, and which must remain a high-water mark in the record of the professions, at least, of the American people:

RESOLVED—That a commission of five members be appointed by the President of the United States to consider the expediency of utilizing existing international agencies for the purpose of limiting the armaments of the nations of the world by international agreement, *and of constituting the combined navies of the world an international force for the preservation of universal peace,* and to consider and report upon any other means to diminish the expenditures of government for military purposes and to lessen the probabilities of war.

What I am pointing out is that nothing remains to be *said* on behalf of the United States in respect to this greatest of all problems. What remains is to *do* something. It is for public opinion to compel members of the legislative branch of the Federal Government to keep the pledges which their several parties have made to the American people.

One has only to lift his eyes from the ground to see that the path which our government should quickly follow lies open before it. The Permanent Court of International Justice at The Hague, originally brought into being by the leadership of the American government, will naturally be the judicial branch and organ of a newly organized or reorganized family or society of nations. The League of Nations at Geneva is the natural point of beginning for that reorganization and readjustment which the past twenty years have shown to be essential in order that it may become the consultative and legisla-tive center of that form of federal union or grouping of nations which has simply got to come into being. The reorganization of the League of Nations must be such as to separate it completely from the Treaty of Versailles and from any unqualified defense of the *status quo* in Europe.

The lesson taught by the League of Nations since its history began is that it was without the power to provide an effective police force to preserve order in the world out upon which it looked. Even the most law-abiding of peoples require a trained and ready police to meet those emergencies which no one can foresee and which, if not met, become invitations to new disorder and new crime. The resolution of the Congress of the United States passed in June, 1910, clearly grasped this fact and pre-sented it to our country and to the world. That fact re-mains as fundamental and as incontrovertible today as it was then.

If the government of the United States has the good faith and the courage to go forward with this leadership, it will find that the very first problems to be solved are monetary and economic. Peace of mind and prosperity cannot be restored to the world until the uncertainties and perplexities which now attach to monetary matters and to trade relations are constructively dealt with. The world does not thrive through international speculation in money. It will thrive if there be established an inter-national monetary standard as definite as the meter and the kilogram. The constant shipment of gold from one

country to another and the present accumulation of some
60 per cent of the world's gold in solitary confinement
in the United States are simply a joke. They mark complete incapacity to deal with one of the most pressing
problems which the world offers, failure to solve which
is a steady temptation to international friction and international ill-will.

Much light will be thrown upon the whole problem
of building an international stabilized monetary system
by study of the history of the Latin Monetary Union,
established in 1865 through the co-operation of France,
Belgium, Switzerland, Italy and Greece. This Union
lasted for some sixty years. The causes of its discontinuance are as illuminating as are those which led to its
organization.[4]

Together with the establishment of a fixed international monetary standard, international trade relationships must be dealt with, and promptly. The spread of
violent and predatory economic nationalism is certainly
the chief cause of the economic depression which holds
the whole world in its grip. Indeed, this has come down
from economic nationalism to economic localism to such
an extent that one would suppose it to be wrong to buy
anything whatever not produced by the community in
which one lives. Even the states of the American Union
are, in flat violation of the provisions of the Federal
Constitution, finding ways to levy taxes which are, in
effect, taxes on imports from other states. The fact that

[4]Willis, Henry Parker, *A History of the Latin Monetary Union: A
Study of International Monetary Action* (University of Chicago Press:
1901) 332 pp.

Fourtens, Bernard, *La fin de l'union monétaire latine* (Paris, 1930)
175 pp.

these are taxes on imports is concealed by their form, but they are none the less the forbidden import taxes. They are as harmful and as dangerous as they are anti-constitutional. Unless this practice be promptly stopped by court action or legislative discontinuance, the federal system in the United States will receive a severe and wholly unexpected blow.

On the other hand, compacts between the states, which are permitted by the Federal Constitution provided they have the approval of the Congress, are increasing in number and are exceedingly helpful. These compacts prove once more the elasticity of a properly organized federal system. Since 1935 thirty-six states, beginning with New Jersey, have set up permanent commissions for interstate co-operation. Some of the more important compacts now in effective operation are those which established the Port of New York Authority, Colorado River Control, Jurisdiction over Oregon-Washington Fisheries, the Palisades Park Agreement and the New York-Vermont Bridge Agreement. It may well be that in the United States this movement within the framework of the Federal Constitution will grow steadily in significance and usefulness.

For five years past, Secretary Hull and his associates in the Department of State have been patiently and persuasively at work reducing the trade barriers which so grievously affect American industry, transportation and commerce. While much has been done, much more yet remains to be done, and through an organized society of nations, established in conformity with those sound federal principles which would be applicable to a world-wide situation, genuine and rapid progress might well be made. The gain to the people of the United States would be very great.

In addition to the monetary problem and the problem of trade relationships, there are a thousand and one questions of world-wide importance to be constructively dealt with through a federal organization of nations. These affect education and philanthropy, standards of living, social security and protection against dependent old age, the conditions and rewards of manual labor, the public health and many other like topics which call for and must have, not isolated and contradictory, but centralized and uniform treatment. Strong appeal will be made to public opinion everywhere by all that concerns improvement in the standard of living of the mass of any of the world's populations. This improvement is essential to the steady and forward-facing development of international trade relations. It must never be forgotten, however, that it is very misleading to judge the standard of living in terms merely of monetary wage or salary. A wage or salary of $50 a day is very inadequate if the daily cost of living be $49.50. On the other hand, a salary of $5 a day might be very comfortable if the cost of living were $2.50 a day. Monetary wages or salary alone have no significance. They must always be judged in terms of and in comparison with the cost of living. Quite as important as the monetary compensation of the worker are his housing and his physical comfort and health. Literally enormous progress has been making in respect to these questions all over the world. In the large cities of the United States, in Great Britain, in Berlin, in Vienna and in Italy, the housing problem has been advanced toward solution by leaps and bounds. No doubt a great deal remains to be done, but men have learned now how to do it.

In approaching all the pressing international problems which deal with money and with trade, the world of today could have no better guidance than that given by Alexander Hamilton in his epoch-making *Papers on Public Credit, Commerce and Finance*,[5] written while Secretary of the Treasury of the United States in 1790, 1791 and 1795. Hamilton saw clearly the ways in which public credit and manufactures might be most wisely and most helpfully built up, as well as the ways in which they might be harmed by undue government interference and control. The wisdom of those great Public Papers is as pronounced today as when they were written. Nothing could be more contrary to fact than to cite Hamilton as the creator or, indeed, as even a defender of the present system of excessively high protective tariffs, which is one of the chief manifestations of that economic nationalism which is wrecking the prosperity of the world and day by day endangering its peace. Why the United States should become a manufacturing nation and how it might become so were plainly demonstrated by Hamilton, but in terms of the freest possible trade for the very obvious reasons which he was careful to set out in detail. It is no exaggeration to say that if the world could produce another Alexander Hamilton, with the vision, the knowledge and the persuasive eloquence to

[5]*Papers on Public Credit, Commerce and Finance, by Alexander Hamilton*, edited by Samuel McKee, Jr. (New York: Columbia University Press, 1934). 302 pp.

do for it what Hamilton did for the American people a
century and a half ago, some, at least, of the world's
troubles would be at an end.

When one observes those troubles and reflects upon
them and their obvious causes, he is tempted to ask
whether perhaps modern man has not grown tired of
civilization and become bored by it. There are not a few
happenings which would lead one to think so. We are
surrounded in every land by clamorous and vigorous
radicals who have no knowledge of the past and whose
only concern for the future is that it shall be as different
as possible from the present. All radicals are reaction-
aries. Their aim is to tear up everything by the roots,
to destroy all that has been done and to begin everything
all over again. Such a program is as unintelligent and
as unpractical as it is dangerous.

A liberal is just the opposite of a radical. A liberal is
one who builds upon the foundation of what has been
accomplished through the centuries in a growing and
widening and deepening civilization, and who goes forward in an open-minded, constructive spirit to guide the
development of all this so that it will serve man's highest and finest needs and ideals, and be kept in conformity
with changing facts and new needs.

There is every sign that if the world is to be turned
over to the radicals it will for an indefinite period be a
regimented and government-controlled world, ruled by
force, either economic or military or both. If the liberal
is to rule, then the world will be one of steady progress
toward carrying economic, social and political liberty
forward to a still higher plane of excellence and practical human service. Man's highest and finest needs and

ideals would then be recognized and, so far as human power goes, met. The choice of today, which will determine the character of the world of tomorrow, is between the radical and the liberal.

An evidence that even a wise man does not always see the end of things is found in the title of a volume by the distinguished English historian, Edward A. Freeman. The full title of that work reads: *History of Federal Government from the Foundation of the Achaian League to the Disruption of the United States, Volume I.* Needless to say, this work was published in 1863, when the American Civil War was at its height. Volume II never appeared.

May it not perhaps be that the failure which now seems to have attended all the recent noble projects for a federal world is not as complete as radical observers would have us believe, and that Volume II of their history of that failure will never be written?

III

LOOKING FORWARD—1938

An article written for *The Argonaut*,
San Francisco, California,
January 1, 1938

LOOKING FORWARD—1938

The year 1937 has been one of the darkest in the whole history of modern civilization. This is due mainly to two causes. The first is an almost complete collapse of public morals, as evidenced by the action of many governments, and the second is man's obvious inability to adjust his daily life—industrial, social and political— to the revolutionary changes which have been brought about through scientific discovery and the consequent vastly increased control over the forces of nature. What we have been witnessing is a world-wide demonstration of moral and intellectual incompetence.

The plighted faith of governments has come to mean nothing, for the words of international treaties are obviously too often written in water. The fundamental principles underlying a civilization built upon civil, economic and political liberty are not only challenged but flatly contradicted. We are asked to accept the preposterous belief that men are perpetually at war with each other through the existence of fixed and definite social and industrial classes whose interests necessarily conflict, instead of being, as we have believed for hundreds of years, members of a steadily growing, free society in which each individual is invited to exert himself to the utmost, not only that he may strengthen his own place in the world, but that he may better serve his fellow men.

The allegory of the Tower of Babel contains in all

essentials the history of mankind. Whatever may have
been the happening which caused the dispersion, the
fact is that from such unity as must have existed at the
very beginning of the life of the human race, there came
with relative speed the great variety of languages and
of interests, and the changes in physical and mental
characteristics, which caused the division of men into
races. Having been divided into races, men shortly began to build nations. The whole known history of mankind is the story of the building of nations.

The outstanding problem before this world today is
to try to learn that a nation is not and cannot be an end
in itself, but that it is a means to an end. There is no
nation large enough, powerful enough, rich enough or
sufficiently self-contained to include the whole of the
human race or to enable its own people best to express
themselves and to take fullest advantage of the opportunities which life has to offer. In looking forward, our
aim is to guide this tendency in nation-building so that
each nation, whether it be great or small, shall regard itself, not as an ultimate end, but as a means, co-operating
with other nations, to advance the happiness, the satisfaction, the prosperity and the contentment of mankind.

When nations are at war it is because they have not
learned the lesson of history and because, whatever their
professions and their excuses, they are facing backward,
not forward. No nation need be large or rich to be
great. One has only to look back at ancient Greece to
find the fullest contradiction of that presumption. In
the world of today it is through our thirst for knowledge
and our guided zeal for the satisfaction of personal and
intellectual ideals, that we discover the meaning of

national companionship, of national co-operation and of common national effort to promote what is finest and best in the life of man.

Close, permanent and well ordered co-operation between nations is of vital importance. Neutrality in the presence of an issue between right and wrong is immoral. Attempted isolation from the welfare and happiness of one's fellow men is immoral. The question, Am I my brother's keeper? was asked and answered long ago.

The peace and the happiness of the world are in the hands of the people and the government of the United States. Will they lead?

IV

THE HIGHER AIM OF HUMAN ACHIEVEMENT

A world-wide broadcast address delivered at the opening
of the new World Headquarters Building of the
International Business Machines Corporation,
New York, January 18, 1938

THE HIGHER AIM OF HUMAN ACHIEVEMENT

Christopher Columbus discovered a new world and became thereby forever famous. Millions upon millions of human beings now living are almost daily discovering a still newer world, but they are far too many to have their names recorded in history. Amazing as were the new knowledge and new ambitions brought to the world of five centuries ago by the vision and courage of Columbus, these fade into insignificance in contrast to the new knowledge and new ambitions which have enriched and are daily enriching the world in which we live. The sources of all that which is so new and so amazing are, first, man's vastly increased knowledge in the field of science and, second, his resulting control in hundreds of new and unforeseen ways of the forces of nature. It is only seven hundred years since Roger Bacon began his career as zealous student and investigator of nature. It is only four hundred years since Copernicus laid the foundations of modern astronomy; while the names of Sir Isaac Newton, of Charles Darwin and of Louis Pasteur seem to belong to the world of but yesterday.

It is my own vivid memory to have been taken as a child to the Centennial Exposition at Philadelphia in 1876 to see the first electric light of Thomas A. Edison and the first telephone of Alexander Graham Bell. It is also a vivid memory to have gone some twenty years

later to the banks of the Potomac River with Professor
Samuel P. Langley and a company of his friends to
witness his first successful experiments to prove that air
flight was possible. Within a very few years thereafter
the Wright brothers made their conclusive demonstration of the practicability of air flight at Kitty Hawk in
North Carolina. Who could possibly imagine that the
electric light, the telephone and the airplane, upon which
the comfort and the convenience of present-day life so
largely depend, are the creation of the few years em-
braced in the span of a single lifetime? The old world
of our fathers and forefathers has disappeared, and its
place has been taken by this new world to which we are
not yet accustomed and of whose characteristics and possibilities we continue to show ourselves strangely igno-
rant.

In the relationships between men and nations, time
and space have disappeared as obstacles or causes of
separation. The electric spark has brought that about.
This new world, however separate its various parts or
units may think themselves, is in fact single and interdependent and will be able to continue to exist only if
that fundamental fact be recognized in thought and in
public policy.

The occasion of our coming together today is to recognize the importance of a great American undertaking
which is conceived and projected in terms of the real
world in which we live. What is a machine? A machine
is defined as any device, whether simple or complex, by
which the intensity of an applied force is increased, its
direction changed, or one form of motion or energy put
into another form. The efficiency of a machine is meas-

ured by the work it is able to accomplish in the face of friction and over the obstacle of distance. Therefore a machine is plainly an instrument of fundamental importance in the life of the world of which we are a part. And what is business? Business, we are told, is the state of being busily engaged in anything, but it has come more specifically to mean personal action which occupies time, demands attention and labor and is in contrast to mere pleasure or recreation. Business is serious employment as distinguished from a pastime. It is an easy matter therefore to gain an understanding of what is meant by the term business machine.

And what is the meaning of the word international? The answer to that question, however simple it be made, rests upon a deep philosophy of human life and human conduct. It signifies that men are grouped together in different geographic homes as a result of historic happenings and traditions which grow out of similarities and differences of race, of language, of religion and of social and political institutions. It means that each one of these has a right to exist in its own way and for the achievement of its own ideals. It means, however, that no one of them is an end in itself but a way to the larger end of human achievement, human co-operation and human satisfaction. Therefore an international business machine is a true representative of the principles underlying our present-day world and, if wisely managed, may easily become a most important influence toward increasing human satisfaction and strengthening the foundations of human confidence and human co-operation upon which alone can rest a permanent peace in this twentieth-century world.

There can be no greater error than to suppose that business is to be conducted for gain alone at no matter what cost in principle, in moral ideals or in human service. Gain-seeking is not in itself to be derided or attacked unless it be gain-seeking undertaken otherwise than in subordination to moral principles and to a spirit of service. Given these presuppositions, then gain-seeking is not only defensible but commendable, whereas without those presuppositions it would be indefensible.

It is these principles and ideals which the twentieth-century world must grasp and act upon if it is to be lifted out of its present maelstrom of lack of confidence, of depression and of antagonism to the very point of military war. The economic war which is everywhere waging is only military war fought with other implements than tanks and guns and poison gas and battleships. It is quite as destructive as military war, and, if it is continued much longer, will certainly bring tumbling to the ground many of those institutions and ideals in which we Americans so profoundly believe. Take down the barriers of international trade. Provide a stabilized and definite monetary standard to serve as the international unit of value and currency measurement, and open men's eyes to the fact that their economic interests, like their moral interests, are common, not antagonistic, and that only through multiplication of acts and policies of human co-operation, human confidence and human action can the world be advanced or even protected in its present stage of development. Words, however eloquent and charming, are idle and futile in the presence of facts and policies which contradict them. We may no longer postpone ceasing to preach prosperity, peace and high human ideals while doing everything in the field of action and public policy to contradict our rhetorical professions and to make the achievement of these ends impossible.

V

THE ABDICATION OF DEMOCRACY

An address delivered at the 184th Commencement
of Columbia University,
June 1, 1938

THE ABDICATION OF DEMOCRACY

Ideas and principles, as well as kings, can abdicate. There are many disturbing signs—and not in Europe or in Asia alone—that Democracy is moving, in no small measure unconsciously, toward abdication. The long and steady progress of democratic principles and ideals which had continued for some three hundred years and which the great World War was to defend and to establish firmly forever, has all too plainly been brought to a halt. By those peoples who have so quickly and so eagerly accepted the rule of dictators and who are just now enthusiastically engaged in upholding and applauding the grotesque and the untrue, Democracy is treated as though it were a sorry and abandoned relic of a day long since gone by. The most fantastic outgivings by dictators and their cheering mobs are hailed as though they were new discoveries in the world of highest intelligence.

Not so long ago that public official whose proud business it is to control and to discipline the German press announced to a welcoming audience that no such thing as individual liberty exists. "There is no freedom of the individual," he cried; "there is only freedom of peoples, nations or races, for these are the only material and historical realities through which the life of the individual exists."[1] The astounding assumption of this speaker was that so-called individuals are not even realities, but merely facets of some community, such as a race or a

[1]Berlin dispatch, *The New York Times*, December 10, 1937.

nation. How can this unutterable nonsense be politely described? Evidently, this thoroughly modern ex- pounder of the absurd had never heard of Goethe's un- answerable dictum: "Mankind? It is an abstraction. There are, always have been, and always will be, men and only men."[2]

It would, indeed, be interesting to go back over the history of mankind and watch a primeval nation or race, without any individuals to compose it, as it evolved out of itself, in the absence of parentage, the original in- dividuals of history! Imagine, if you can, a world popu- lated only by totalitarian communities producing from its inchoate mass and by its own lofty intellectual and spiritual power, an Abraham or a Moses, a Socrates or a Plato, a Cæsar or a Cicero, a Dante or a Petrarch, a Descartes or a Bossuet, a Shakespeare or a Milton, a Goethe or a Schiller, a Washington or a Hamilton! One hardly knows how to characterize such preposterous imaginings and yet they underlie—if not in so blunt and self-contradictory a form—much of what is being said and urged and done all over the world of today. These enthusiastic devotees of the untrue might well reflect upon Nietzsche's dictum: "The coldest of all cold monsters is called the State. . . . This coldest of all lies crawls from its mouth: I, the State, am the people."

How often must it be repeated that Democracy rests upon moral principles and that only when these are recognized and supported does it concern itself with the purely material interests of individuals and of groups?

[2]Goethe mit Heinrich Luden, August 19, 1806, *Goethes Gespraeche* (Leipzig, 1889), II, 83.

The individual human being whose life and conduct are inspired by an understanding of moral principles will not impose upon his fellow man, nor will he take part in depriving that fellow man of any of the vast and many-sided opportunity which life may offer to him. The chief problem of Democracy, if it is to be successful and continuing, is the moral education and guidance of the individual and not the suppression of the individual in the supposed interest of some mass or group. If Democracy be worthy and true to its aim, then the abler, the richer, the more successful the individual, the abler, the richer, the more successful will the entire democratic state become. It is the imperfection and moral dereliction of mankind which trouble Democracy, which attempt to divide the state into permanent conflicting groups or classes, and which prevent Democracy's advance, rather than any unsoundness of the principles on which Democracy rests. When that state which is democratic in form accepts the doctrine of permanent conflicting classes, the abdication of Democracy has begun.

Democracy may choose any one of several forms of political organization and effective administration. It may choose the monarchic form, as in Great Britain and in Sweden. It may choose the republican form, as in France and the United States. Or it may, very infrequently and under very unusual circumstances of geography and population, choose direct democracy. For obvious reasons the democratic monarchy and the democratic republic are the most efficient forms of Democracy's political organization, but neither form will work itself. The democratic state is confronted day by day with precisely the same moral problems and duties which confront the individual citizen in a Democracy. If the democratic state insists upon making it permanent policy to engage in war—whether that war be military or economic or political—then it is paving the way for its own destruction, since in war dictatorship instantly asserts itself, either in political form or under the guise of military necessity. Therefore the only hope of a continued and strengthened Democracy is the avoidance of war by the prevention of war and by the removal of the causes of war.

No one of these very practical ends can be accomplished by yielding to the threats of dictators, or by accepting the challenge which dictators offer in the form of written pledges which they have no intention to keep if found to be in conflict with what are called their interests. Therefore in this highly practical world there is a point at which the rule of force may be needed in order that Democracy can survive, just as in any modern community there is need of police in order that riots and personal assaults may be prevented and punished. In a perfect community there would be no need of police, and in a perfect world there will be no need of force. Until, however, the world approaches perfection in higher degree than has yet been the case, there must be force in reserve—moral force, political force, economic force and, in last and unwelcome resort, even military force—if progress toward greater liberty, greater fairness and larger opportunity for all men is to be effectively protected.

There is nothing new in all this. It is less than a century and a quarter since Napoleon Bonaparte was marching from one end of Europe to the other and

Austerlitz, Waterloo and St. Helena were familiar names.

Just now three powerful dictatorships have bluffed the democracies into giving aid to the crippling of the one hopeful and progressive institution which modern man has brought into existence to make possible that constant and effective international consultation and international action, on the part of small nations as well as great, which alone can lay the foundations for a prosperous and a peaceful world in which Democracy may live and grow and serve. Those dictatorships have forced a return to that old and fatal system of group alliances between nations which contemplate war, which at huge and destructive cost unceasingly prepare for war and which end in war.

When Democracy fails to realize these fundamental facts and to act upon them, it abdicates. It turns over the rule of the world to cruel and relentless force wielded by dictators, and it offers dictatorship a subtle but inviting opportunity to enter its own territory and to overturn the very institutions whose excellence it continues to acclaim. If Democracy is to continue in any form, it must assert the power which belongs to it as a great ruler. It must exert that power through whatever agencies it establishes, whether monarchic or republican, in the field of political organization, in the field of economic policy and even, if need there be, in the field of military force. The alternative is the abdication of Democracy.

Can it be possible that Spengler was right when he told the world some twenty years ago that the decline of the west was obvious and certain? Must the coming generation accept a situation in which Democracy, through feebleness, lack of moral courage and want of efficiency, becomes "the spectator of its own tragedy rather than the hero of its own destiny?"

VI

THE UNITED STATES MUST LEAD

An address delivered before The American Club of Paris
at the Cercle Interallié,
June 14, 1938

THE UNITED STATES MUST LEAD

The greetings of the French Government and those of the Universities of France were presented by M. Jean Zay, Minister of Public Instruction and the Fine Arts.

Monsieur le Ministre: For the distinction and the honor of your presence and your words, so cordial, of greeting and good will, I offer an expression of my grateful thanks and appreciation. My personal links with the life, the thought and the education of France go back, Monsieur le Ministre, over more than half a century. Those years are full of recognition of the joy, the satisfaction and the profit of the highest type which they have brought to my intellectual and personal life. I thank you.

Mr. President, my friends of The American Club and your distinguished guests:

This greeting which you offer me year by year means very much to me and gives me a new sense of the significance of the French people, their life and their achievements for those of us who live in other parts of the world. I can bring you from across the Atlantic a message of greeting from your fellow Americans and of good will, but I cannot quite say what was said to President Lincoln by the General in command of his troops, that "All is quiet on the Potomac." All is not quiet on the Potomac, any more than it is quiet anywhere else.

The world, particularly the American world, is slowly awakening to the fact that under these twentieth-century conditions nothing of importance can happen to any people on any continent without having some effect, and often very great effect, on every other people on earth. Ten days ago, in speaking to the State Bar Association at Nashville, Tennessee, Mr. Secretary Cordell Hull made the most significant, the most forward-facing and the most constructive speech which has been made by any public officer in the United States since 1920. It may well be that that speech is to mark a turning-point in this epoch of world history. Let me read to you two short passages:

It is my firm conviction that national isolation is not a means to security, but rather a fruitful source of insecurity. For while we may seek to withdraw from participation in world affairs, we cannot thereby withdraw from the world itself. Attempts to achieve national isolation would not merely deprive us of any influence in the councils of nations, but would impair our ability to control our own affairs. . . .

Solemn contractual obligations are brushed aside with a light heart and a contemptuous gesture. Respect for law and observance of the pledged word have sunk to an inconceivably low level. The outworn slogans of the glorification of war are again resounding in many portions of the globe. Armed force, naked and unashamed, is again being used as an instrument of policy and a means of attaining national ends through aggression and aggrandizement. It is being employed with brutality and savagery that outrage and shock every humane instinct.

There is desperate need in our country, and in every country, of a strong and united public opinion in support of such a renewal and demonstration of faith in the possibility of a world order based on law and international co-operative effort.

There speaks the statesman looking facts in the face, turning his back upon empty and meaningless formulas and facing the future with insight and with courage. But there is no time to be lost. The familiar public policy of Wait and See will not do. The time has come for quick, courageous and constructive leadership, and it is possible now for the American people, in the spirit of that declaration, to offer it, both to their own advantage and for the rebuilding of the broken foundations of world prosperity and world peace.

Mr. Chairman, that is the traditional American policy and has been so for one hundred and seventy years. There is a superstition, repeated time and time again, that our traditional policy is one of isolation. That superstition is contradicted by every fact in American history from the time of Benjamin Franklin to the present day. We have not only never been isolated but we have sought every opportunity to explain our life, our institutions, our ideals to peoples in other parts of the world, and particularly to the peoples of France and of Great Britain. What was Benjamin Franklin doing while spending twenty-two years of his life in Paris and in London? What was Thomas Jefferson, author of the Declaration of Independence, doing when sitting in the gallery at Versailles yonder and listening to the debate on the Declaration of the Rights of Man? What was John Adams doing, living in London and explaining the new Federal Constitution to the British people? What was being done by our great constructive Secretaries of State from that time almost to this—John Quincy Adams, Daniel Webster, William H. Seward, Hamilton Fish and Elihu Root, every one of them a powerful force in the affairs of the whole world, every one of them offering helpful co-operation, constructive criticism and guidance on behalf of the American people?

If by a policy of isolation is meant that our people intend at every possible cost to refrain from war, well and good; but that is not isolation: it is something quite different. We are now dealing with the real underlying forces, forces of thought, forces of opinion—the forces which move men in their social, economic and political life.

It is habitual with certain of our public men who hail isolation as a policy to quote a sentence from President Washington's Farewell Address and another sentence from Thomas Jefferson's first inaugural. Indeed, what they usually do is to quote the sentence from Jefferson's first inaugural and ascribe it to Washington's Farewell Address. Both men were effective exponents of the policy of international collaboration and co-operation, and what those two sentences meant was a warning not to become involved in the Napoleonic Wars, which some years later we managed to do in the form of the War of 1812. We do not realize how powerful has been the movement among our people not only to co-operate in maintaining prosperity and peace, but in offering leadership and guidance and counsel to that end. Run your eye back over the history of the last forty years. It is a little more than forty years since there was issued in the name of the Czar of All the Russias the most extraordinary appeal to other governments that the world has ever heard. It is a classic document entitled to rank with the very highest, inviting those governments to come forth and counsel together as to ways and means of collaborating to preserve the peace of the world. The result was the first Hague Conference of 1899. President McKinley rejoiced at the possibility of accepting this invitation and sent to that Conference a delegation of outstanding Americans, at whose head was Andrew D. White, statesman and educator. It was the American delegation which saved that Conference from hopeless failure, because, when the governments could not agree upon some of the larger phases of the questions submitted to them, it was the American delegation which proposed that they should agree upon bringing into existence a permanent court of arbitration. That was done. The court was set up and in a year or two it began to function. Next came the invitation of 1908. Read Mr. Secretary Root's letter of instruction to the American delegation to that Conference headed by Joseph H. Choate, and you will find a most magnificent and convincing argument for international co-operation in the interests of prosperity and peace.

There is hardly an American who knows how far our public opinion went at that fortunate time, almost exactly twenty-eight years ago. It was on June 4, 1910, that this joint resolution, which I shall read, was on the calendar of the House of Representatives at Washington. And I repeat that probably not one American in a million knows of its existence.

The resolution was to authorize the appointment of a commission in relation to universal peace:

RESOLVED—That a commission of five members be appointed by the President of the United States to consider the expediency of utilizing existing international agencies for the purpose of limiting the armaments of the nations of the world by international agreement, *and of constituting the combined navies of the world an international force for the preservation of universal peace,* and to consider and report upon any other means to diminish the expenditures of government for military purposes and to lessen the probabilities of war.

What happened to that remarkable resolution? It passed the House of Representatives by unanimous consent. It went to the Senate on June 20, and four days following it passed the Senate also by unanimous consent, and was signed by the President of the United States. So the government of the United States was then proposing to lead the way to the establishment of an international police force for the protection of international law and international morality. Was that isolation?

Consider some of the names that are associated with that resolution. The Committee on Foreign Relations in the Senate, which reported it without dissent, included these well-known names: Shelby M. Cullom of Illinois, William P. Frye of Maine, Henry Cabot Lodge of Massachusetts, Clarence D. Clark of Wyoming, John Kean of New Jersey, Albert J. Beveridge of Indiana, Thomas H. Carter of Montana, William Alden Smith of Michigan, Elihu Root of New York. The Committee on Foreign Affairs in the House of Representatives, which also reported it without dissent, included: David J. Foster of Vermont, J. Sloat Fassett of New York, William B. McKinley of Illinois, Frank O. Lowden of Illinois, William S. Bennet of New York, William M. Howard of Georgia, John N. Garner of Texas, now Vice-President of the United States, and Gilbert M. Hitchcock of Nebraska.

There spoke the whole American people. Not Republicans only, not Democrats only. There was not a single dissenting voice. Among those recorded as present, and therefore as voting, were the Senator from Massachusetts who became an arch-isolationist, Mr. Henry Cabot Lodge, and also the Crown Prince of isolationism, Mr. Borah of Idaho.

What happened?

In his message to the Congress in the following December, President Taft wrote:

> Appreciating these enlightened tendencies of modern times, the Congress at its last session passed a law providing for the appointment of a commission of five members "to be appointed by the President of the United States to consider the expediency of utilizing existing international agencies for the purpose of limiting the armaments of the nations of the world by international agreement, and of constituting the combined navies of the world an international force for the preservation of universal peace, and to consider and report upon any other means to diminish the expenditures of government for military purposes and to lessen the probabilities of war."
>
> I have not yet made appointments to this commission because I have invited and am awaiting the expressions of foreign governments as to their willingness to co-operate with us in the appointment of similar commissions or representatives who would meet with our commissioners and by joint action seek to make their work effective.

It is of record in the Department of State that Mr. Taft sounded out the governments of Europe, and that the governments of Germany, of Austria, of France and of Great Britain, while expressing sympathy, said that the time was not ripe, that there were too many chances of disturbance and of danger and that it would

be wise to defer action. Action was deferred and the
fatal August, 1914, soon followed. Once again it was
the disastrous policy of Wait and See.

It is vitally important, Mr. Chairman, not only for
Americans but for the whole civilized world to realize
what our people and our government were unanimously
prepared to do then, and to bring them back to be prepared to do it now.

Great progress was made, although by different methods and in various directions, between 1919 and 1929.
Steps were taken now here, now there, to improve international relations and international conditions. I shall
always believe the untimely death, first of Doctor
Stresemann and then of M. Briand, to be largely responsible for checking the constructive movement which
was then going forward. Immediately thereafter came
the world economic and monetary crisis in which we still
live and which holds every nation in its grasp. It is a
complete illusion to think that there is a French crisis
and a German crisis and an English crisis and an American crisis and an Argentine crisis. There is a world
crisis, which expresses itself under different conditions
and limitations in each country, but at bottom the causes
and their effects are absolutely one and the same.

Understanding those facts and looking them in the
face, why have we not been able to make progress in
solving these questions? Why is it that the world is
going on using up the savings of a thousand years and
borrowing as against the possible savings of generations
to come? Why is it that we have been unable thus far
in any considerable degree to co-operate to check the
growth of these destructive forces, economic and social,

every one of which makes for the undermining of prosperity and for temptation to destroy peace? Why is it?

There met in London, at Chatham House, in March, 1935, sixty-two of the leading personalities of the world, statesmen, economists, bankers, industrialists, diplomats, coming from ten countries. They spent days in intimate consultation as to how to answer the question which I am now asking. To the great surprise of themselves as well as of every one else, those sixty-two men, with different backgrounds and different points of view, agreed unanimously upon a program of economic and monetary reform. That program, simple and easily understood, has been enthusiastically accepted by the International Chamber of Commerce and by the Carnegie Endowment for International Peace, and those two bodies are now working day and night in their quiet way to press it upon the attention of the public and of the governments in order to stop the policy of Wait and See and to get something done. Any observer of human nature and of government must know that the longer we Wait and See, the more ammunition we present to dictatorship in whatever form it may show itself. There comes a time when men are perfectly hopeless, when they must get something done. If they cannot do it, if their governments cannot do it, who is it that can do it? That is the history of every dictatorship for a thousand or fifteen hundred years. The German philosopher Hegel said a great many wise things, but one of the wisest was this: "We ask men to study history. The only thing that man learns from the study of history is that men have learned nothing from the study of history."

We permit these forces to repeat themselves generation after generation, century after century. We look at them as if they were utterly new, as if the world had never heard of them before; and yet in one way or another, from the time of ancient Egypt, man has had to deal with this problem in some one of its forms. All this has been enormously accentuated and emphasized in our time by the stage which has been reached in the history of nation-building. Nation-building began when the Roman Empire fell. Up to that time it was man's conception that a single force or power might control the whole world and rule it. This started Alexander the Great to Asia and Cæsar to France and Great Britain. That attempt went on for hundreds of years, and then, when it broke down, men began building nations in Europe. The ideal definition of a nation is an ethnic unity which inhabits a geographic unity. There is no pure ethnic unity and, I suppose, few complete geographic unities; but the definition is intended to guide our thinking. Men have been seeking to bring their own language, their own inheritance, their own religion, together into one social order and government and then to make it safe and comfortable by gaining for it control of a geographic unity. On your map you see at once that Italy is a perfect geographic unity with the Alps and the Adriatic Sea on the north and east and the Mediterranean on the south and west. The Iberian Peninsula is a perfect geographic unity, with the Pyrenees and the Atlantic Ocean on the north and west and the Strait of Gibraltar and the Mediterranean on the south and east. The British Islands are a perfect geographic unity. The Scandinavian countries are a geographic unity. Here on the Continent, in Central and Eastern Europe, the mountains are not high enough and the rivers are not broad enough to have indicated where the ethnic unity might end its growth, and as a result you have had a thousand years of wars.

That is a very concrete and a very definite problem. We are face to face with that and it can only be solved in one of two ways. If I may contradict myself, the first way will not solve it. It may be solved by force, which means a temporary solution only, or it may be solved by reason. The minorities problem is not new. Fortunately, France has been very little troubled with it. But look at Great Britain: Angles, Saxons, Danes, Normans, Scots, Celts. War after war for five hundred years and then finally they found a solution. They can all live in peace and quiet and order together. We in America have had a very grave minorities problem with our colored people. It led to a vast Civil War which almost disrupted the nation, and it took seventy years before it came to that climax. So, when you see these minorities problems elsewhere, in Asia, in Africa, in Eastern Europe, do not forget that we have had no end of experience with that problem and that there are only the two ways of dealing with it: by force, which does not settle it, and by reason, which will settle it. Time, good order, kindly feeling, high-mindedness, moral standards and faith in human nature are necessary.

As one goes about the world today, he must be impressed with the discouragement which is felt everywhere. In America, and here in Europe, almost the first word following a greeting is one of discouragement and despair, as to the monetary, the economic, the social, the political, and even the peace outlook. But, my friends, that is not the way to solve anything. Pessimism is the last resource of the coward. Optimism, faith in mankind, belief in ideas, courage and willingness to call upon your fellow men to come up out of their little narrow personal environments and to show themselves citizens of their nations and of the world, constitute a constructive force that, instead of making this twentieth century of ours the end of an era, will show that we have been able to make it the beginning of a new order in a peaceful and a prosperous world.

VII

LA SOCIÉTÉ DES NATIONS

An article written for the Agence Littéraire
Internationale, Paris, July 21, 1938

LA SOCIÉTÉ DES NATIONS

The obvious fact that the electric spark and its application have brought into existence a wholly new world has not yet been grasped by the mass of mankind. They continue to think and to act as if the world of Louis XIV or that of the French Revolution or even that of the foundation of the Third Republic were still in existence. Those worlds have all disappeared forever. Their place has been taken by a world in which neither time nor space imposes any limitations upon the spread of knowledge, the growth of trade or the march of political and economic principles and ideals. It is only two generations since Jules Verne startled the world by taking as the title for one of his popular books *Around the World in Eighty Days.* We have just now seen a trip around the world made in less than four days. What happens in Paris, in London or in New York today, if it be important, is known in Argentina, in Australia and in Japan almost immediately. The barriers of language have been beaten down and the demonstrated truths of modern science speak in no single tongue. What is the meaning, the deeper significance, of these amazing and as yet little appreciated facts?

My answer to this question is that in order to continue to progress or even to exist the civilized world must adapt its thinking and also its political, its economic and its social organization to meet these new conditions of existence here on earth. The world is one, and mankind must recognize that fact and act accordingly. This does not mean that all men are to be brought under one government or one form of political, social and economic organization. Far from it. What it does mean, however, is that nations having different historic backgrounds, speaking different languages, living under different climates and preferring different political, economic and social forms of organization must, while preserving these characteristic differences, recognize their community of interest and of purpose. This can only be done by a new adaptation of the principle of federal organization. That principle, which was adopted by Bismarck when he organized the German Empire in 1871, has found its outstanding examples and manifestations in the Constitution of the United States of America, now one hundred and fifty years old, and in the Statute of Westminster, by which in 1931 the British Commonwealth of Nations was brought into being in its present extraordinarily successful form. These well-known and well-recognized examples of the success of the federal principle point the way to that new system of world organization for the establishment of prosperity and the maintenance of progress and of peace for which the whole world is waiting.

Woodrow Wilson and those who were associated with him in bringing into existence the League of Nations had a great vision, but by incorporating the constitution of that League in a treaty which dealt with conditions growing out of the great World War, both its permanent establishment and quick success were made extremely difficult. This is why more progress has not been made since 1919 in reorganizing the broken world. Unhappily, we were deprived of the leadership of Stresemann and Briand far too soon. Then came the severe and world-wide economic and financial crisis, which multiplied all our problems and difficulties.

Nevertheless, the great work of world organization must go on, with Geneva as its capital and with The Hague as the seat of its highest Court of International Justice. The phrase used in the Treaty of Versailles was "La Société des Nations," and it was a distinct misfortune that in English this phrase was translated the League of Nations. There were many who felt that the term League meant that the nations were to organize for something or against something and therefore they resisted such organization. On the other hand, La Société des Nations, the Family of Nations, is a persuasive and inviting term. Following the example of the Constitution of the United States and that of the Statute of Westminster, the time has fully come when the colossal damage wrought by the mistakes and happenings of the past twenty years must be brought to an end and their recurrence made impossible by a world-wide federal organization of the Family of Nations. All the good things that have been accomplished at Geneva, and they are many, can and should be emphasized and retained. The nations must go beyond what has already been done and place in the hands of a duly constituted federal authority certain definitely prescribed and delegated powers representative of that world unity which is so obvious and so imperative.

There is no longer any such thing as a sovereign nation in the sense that a nation may do what it pleases, as it pleases, when it pleases. Human knowledge and human morality have proceeded far beyond that point. The moral law is sovereign, and to that moral law every nation which pretends to be civilized must give obedience. Let that fact be recognized, and an effective organization of the Family of Nations in a new and convincing application of the federal principle can go forward, and the burdens which now rest upon mankind everywhere be quickly lightened and lifted. Let the word Geneva mean for the generations to come what the words Paris and London and Washington mean for those peoples whose capitals and symbols of unity they are.

VIII

DEMOCRACY IN DANGER

An address delivered at the Parrish Art Museum,
Southampton, Long Island,
September 4, 1938

DEMOCRACY IN DANGER

"Where there is no vision, the people perish." These words were spoken some three thousand years ago and from that day to this their wisdom has been shown over and over again in the history of the human race. In rising from the animal to the human being, and from the lower stages of human existence to the higher, men have persistently remained to a very large degree under the domination of the characteristics of that lower order out of which their natures were developing. In part this is something easily understood, because no matter how high one rises in the scale of human accomplishment and human attributes, yet there always remain to be dealt with those necessities of physical and animal life which go back to the very beginnings of things. To put it differently, that vision of which King Solomon speaks is everywhere and always in competition with those needs and habits which have to do with the maintenance of physical life in all its phases. In this continuing struggle, it is only when vision is attained and when it asserts itself that true progress is made and that life moves forward and onward to a higher plane of endeavor and of achievement. Those who persist in describing this conflict of human motives and moving forces as one between the real and the ideal or between the practical and the theoretical, vision being looked upon as ideal and theoretical, are misusing words. There is nothing more real or more practical than vision, and there is nothing more unreal or more unpractical than to fix one's eyes on the ground under one's feet and never to lift those eyes to see what lies beyond and above. The grave danger which today confronts Democracy is directly due to lack of that understanding which only vision can bring.

The term Democracy is so loosely used as often to prevent any true comprehension of its real meaning. The term is ordinarily defined as government by the People, the Demos; but it is never to be forgotten that precisely the same individuals who constitute the Demos, the People, also constitute the Mob, and that Democracy is not government by the Mob. This is the reason why for any real comprehension of the meaning and principles of a democratic form of government the People must be distinguished from the Mob. The difference between the two ought to be readily observable by any one who watches the habits and the conduct of his fellow human beings. Crowds rushing hither and yon under the impulse of some controlling emotion, whether it be curiosity or cruelty or greed, are the Mob in action. The same individuals hearkening to an elevated and inspiring argument or appeal in the field of literature or of science, of religion or of politics, are the People at their best. The ruling motives in the one case are passion and selfishness, accompanied by ignorance; the ruling motives in the other case are ambition to learn and to understand, with a view to acting on a high intellectual and moral plane and in the largest public interest. To speak bluntly, Democracy cannot possibly exist for any length of time with the Mob in control of its institutions and its policies. Despotism in some one of its familiar forms will speedily come to displace Democracy, and the Mob will acclaim that Despotism as its own familiar friend. History offers only too many illustrations of this fact.

Looking at the present-day world as a whole, it must be borne in mind that while Democracy in thought, in ideal and in practice on a small scale has been well known since the days of ancient Greece, it has come to its flower in Western Europe and in America only during the past century and a half. The many and important peoples of Central and Eastern Europe have never known Democracy save in name and have never made themselves responsible for it over any considerable length of time or in any considerable degree. The peoples of Russia, having a background which is quite as Asiatic as it is European, have always been under the control of a despot, whether that despot be called a Czar or a Communist Commissar. The German people in their political life have always been under strict regimentation, both national and local, and have seemed to prefer it because of the efficiency which it almost always brought in its train. Through all this strict political regimentation, however, the German people, to their great glory and power, kept complete freedom in the field of the intellect and of the arts. Today that freedom, too, is denied them, with disastrous consequences, the full effect of which it is not easy to foretell.

The world of today, all parts of which have been drawn so closely together by the electric spark and the forces which it has unloosed, is finding very great difficulty in understanding itself and in dealing with its problems because of the different attitudes of its various constituent peoples toward Democracy. Every day it becomes more clear that the peoples of Western Europe, particularly the English and the French, and those of America, have been too greatly concerned with their own immediate happenings and history and have not sought to comprehend the states of mind and the problems which are characteristic of the increasingly important peoples of Eastern and Southeastern Europe. The differences of race, of language, of historical tradition and of background which characterize these peoples have been in large part unfamiliar to those nations which during the past century and a half have become the so-called Western Democracies. This explains in large part why the Treaty of Versailles created more problems, both political and economic, than it solved, and why the center of gravity in respect to difficult international relations has now moved so far to the east. That treaty, instead of marking the end of a great war which was to make the world safe for Democracy, opened an era in which Democracy is exposed to more difficulties and dangers than ever before in its history. Not only has the extension of Democracy to peoples hitherto non-democratic been almost entirely checked, but forces have been unloosed which are bringing new dangers to Democracy in nations where its foundations had been thought to be entirely secure.

The stubborn and even violent opposition to Democracy is both political and economic in form and in origin. Upholders and exponents of that new form of political organization which is known as Fascism habitually speak of Democracy with undisguised and unrestrained contempt. They regard it as not dying but dead. This attitude is the expression of the belief that Democracy is of necessity incapable and inefficient, and that highly organized and essentially despotic leadership, which insists upon the so-called totalitarian state, is the only form of political organization which makes national prosperity and national greatness possible. Such a conception, of course, involves arming a people for war and steadily planning war while the despot, with his tongue in his cheek, proclaims himself the greatest possible lover and exponent of world peace.

That collection of organized absurdities and contradictions which has for the time being taken over the control of the great German people under the name of National Socialism differs from Fascism more in form than in fact. National Socialism, too, must have absolute and unquestioning obedience to the ruling despotism, and it must be supported in its appalling racial persecutions, in its economic offenses and in its unparalleled preparations for a war that must rock the world, while it, too, like the Fascist spokesmen, lets no opportunity pass to extol peace, both as an ideal of national policy and as a necessary accompaniment of national greatness and power. It denies to minorities, whether they be racial, linguistic, political, economic or religious, even the right to exist. It is newly enthroned barbarism.

Is it any wonder, when circumstances such as these and their many-sided evidences confront us day by day, that the state of world opinion is at once dominated and rocked by total lack of confidence and by the growing fear that all these crude and passionate contradictions will some day explode and involve mankind in a new and appalling catastrophe?

While this violent attack on Democracy by Fascism and National Socialism is chiefly political in form, yet the economic doctrines which lie behind the political are highly important. In the case of the war on Democracy which Communism, with Russia as its capital, is everywhere waging, the economic motive dominates the political, at least in theory. Doubtless the Lenins and the Stalins would smile at this suggestion, and in their case at least the smile would be justified. The whole Communist agitation, which is well organized and persistently carried on, even among the democratic peoples themselves, is the most obvious and most widespread form of public unmorality that the world has yet witnessed. To call Communism liberal or progressive is to show one's dense ignorance, not only of what those terms mean, but of Communism itself. Communism is an attempted return to barbarism under the driving impulse of envy, hatred and malice. It is envious of any individual or of any group which possesses or has gained excellence, whether it be in the field of public service, of intellectual activity, of artistic endeavor, of industrial planning or of earnings and savings. All must be pulled down to the level of the least competent, and the door of advancement must be closed to ambition, to skill and to zeal for public service.

One has only to read in some detail the story of the life and occupations of Karl Marx in Cologne, in Paris, in Brussels and in London to learn that the guiding stars of his whole activity were envy, hatred and malice. He found material for his outgivings in some of the characteristics of that industrial feudalism which marked the passing of the industrial revolution into a period of industrial evolution, and which were the unfortunate but understandable results of lack of comprehension and lack of understanding of all that the new industrial processes involved for those who took part in them, whether as workers with the hand or as workers with the brain or as participants through their just and careful savings.

It was particularly upon the latter group that the savage attacks of Karl Marx were made. He called them capitalists, intended as a term of abuse, as if to have worked and saved was a crime. The system in which they participated he called capitalism, again directing at that system and at this particular word his malicious abuse and violent slander. He appears never to have grasped the fact that there is not, never has been and never can be any such system as capitalism, since capital is not a principle at all. Capital is simply the by-product of Liberty in the field of work. Capital is what remains to the worker after he has met the cost of his work and of his livelihood. It is for him, in a society of free men, to determine what to do with his savings. He may selfishly spend these upon himself and his pleasures, or he may employ them in the development of some new undertaking in the field of agriculture, of industry, of transportation, of the intellectual or artistic life, which will serve his fellow men, increase their happiness and raise the standards and level of the civilization of which they are a part. He may make this use of his savings either as an individual or in co-operation with other workers who, like himself, have made savings. In such case, he uses his savings in co-operation, probably through a corporation, and a corporation means co-oper-

ation. What, therefore, the Communist is attacking in
Democracy is that Liberty which is its cornerstone. A
direct attack on Liberty would not be very popular and
might easily excite derision. Therefore the words capital, capitalist and capitalism have been invented as representing something which, it is hoped, may be attacked
with a larger measure of public support.

These highly organized and persistently pursued attacks on Democracy, both in the political sphere and in
the economic, by Fascism, by National Socialism and by
Communism, have so much in common that it is not a
wholly unsafe prediction that, despite some of the things
which Fascism and National Socialism on the one hand
and Communism on the other now say of each other,
they may one of these days find themselves in steadily
increasing sympathy and collaboration because of their
hatred of Democracy and their desperate intention to
crush it entirely if that be at all practicable. The steady
weakening of Communist practice in Russia, despite the
continuing upholding of Communist theory, shows that
people to be moving, whether they know it or not, nearer
and nearer to National Socialism. The violent regimentation of everything which now prevails in Germany is
a much closer approximation to Communism than is understood by those who are conducting this regimentation
and at the same time denouncing Communism with great
violence. The steady economic penetration of Germany
into Eastern and Southeastern Europe is for the purpose
of building up a group of economic interdependences
and relationships which in due time will make economic
and military co-operation easy to accomplish.

It may just as well be recognized now as later that the

eastern boundary of Democracy is practically the River
Rhine, for Czechoslovakia, whose people, if freed from
terrorism, would gladly retain their progressive democracy, is the only democratic state left east of that river.
It is at the River Rhine that the line of intellectual,
political and economic battle between Democracy and its
enemies will be drawn. It is doubtless the conscious or
unconscious recognition of that fact which has led to the
building in recent years of those literally appalling military fortifications and installations which line the Rhine
on either bank from Switzerland to the Netherlands.

How is Democracy to meet a crisis such as this? Must
it, too, prepare for war at the cost of all that it holds
most dear, both in morals and in the material aspects
of life, or is there some alternative?

Unhappily, events of the past ten years have made it
pretty plain that the dictators and their totalitarian states
are not open to argument or to moral appeal. In far-
away Japan there is a large and most intelligent element
of the population which is sympathetic with Democracy,
but this element has been stamped under the heel of the
cruel, merciless and highly ambitious military party
which has set out to do for Eastern Asia something like
that which it conceives the English people to have done
for the North American continent. This alone, and
neither peace nor prosperity nor intellectual excellence
nor international co-operation, is for them the mark of
true national greatness.

A world war in this twentieth century between the
Despotisms and the Democracies would put to shame
every war which history records. It could have but one
end, and that would be the destruction of our civiliza-

tion. The long and proud story which begins with ancient Greece and comes down to our own day and generation would be brought to an end with the fatal word *Finis.*

Unless Democracy is to contemplate this tragic end, it must quickly bestir itself. It must cease taking for granted that it is the latest and best of all forms of political and social organization, and must prove it. It must cease contemplating with lazy unconcern those conditions of life, of work, of health and of insecurity and illness and old age which move every truly human heart. It must stop using the institutions and privileges of Democracy for purely personal and selfish and gain-seeking ends and lift itself up to the plane of a life whose greatest joy is the betterment of one's fellow men and of the conditions which face and surround them. In other words, Democracy must prove to this twentieth century that it has the vigor, the capacity, the ideals and the moral courage, not only to justify itself in the eyes of its own people but in due time to convince the despotic peoples themselves that they are on the wrong and backward track, judged even from the standpoint of their own individual and national interests. This war must be one of morals and of intellect.

What Democracy suffers from today is paralysis of will, and there can be no worse political or social disease than that. Democracy lacks those voices of leadership, of imagination and of constructive power which have guided it so often in the past and to which the great body of convinced believers in Democracy so quickly responded. No one seriously debates that something should be done without delay to relieve the world-wide economic depression which is at the basis of the world-wide lack of confidence and which so greatly adds to the power of the dictators. Yet nothing is done by any democratic government. Secretary Hull at Washington and former Prime Minister van Zeeland of Belgium are the two outstanding exceptions, but each is sharply criticized in return for his vision and his constructive statesmanship. Every one deplores war, joins in passing resolutions against war and in making emotional appeals that there be no war, yet preparations for war go on in appalling fashion and the democratic governments have without exception made plans for the complete governmental regimentation of the life and industry of their entire peoples should war come. In other words, by incompetence, by irresolution, by want of leadership and by lack of vision, the great democracies are in effect inviting just that which they so greatly and so justifiably fear.

What has happened to Democracy in these later years of its history? Why is it not producing the powerful and constructive leadership which it so abundantly enjoyed in its earlier years? Why are there no longer in our American official life any names to be mentioned in the same class with the great founders of the republic and the outstanding political leaders of widely varying types and views who distinguished the first century and a quarter of our nation's history? Why is England in similar plight? Where in our time is the successor to Burke or Fox or Pitt, to Peel or Cobden or Gladstone, to Balfour or Asquith? France, too, must search far and long for a present-day Thiers or Gambetta.

There are those who would answer these questions by

the statement that the Western Democracies have, during the past generation, become far too greatly concerned with regional and group interests and advantages, and that the general welfare of all the people, as well as the fundamental principles upon which Democracy rests, have been pushed far into the background.

Democracy as a form of political government has always worked best when the people divided themselves into two opposing parties. One party, the liberal, would wish to march forward, sometimes too fast. The other party, the conservative, would wish to keep things as they are, perhaps too long. When the liberal party went forward so fast that it shook public confidence, the conservative party was put in power to take its place.. When the conservative party resisted change which public opinion felt to be necessary, then it was displaced by the liberal party. The English democracy worked substantially in this way during almost the whole of the nineteenth century and it was effective in high degree. The American democracy worked in the same way in large part but the simplicity of the choice between liberal and conservative was greatly complicated in this country by the pressing problems growing out of the slavery question. In France the people quickly divided themselves into several political parties, and the moment that is done regional and group advantage begin to claim more attention than does the general welfare. So it happens that Democracy weakens itself through not guarding and protecting itself against the invasion of government by individual and group interests at the cost of fundamental principles and the general good.

The people of the United States have had an education in Democracy more effective and more fruitful than that of any other people. This is due to the fact that the principles, the form and the limitations of their federal government were put into a written constitution. There are many other written constitutions in the world, but none which approaches the Constitution of the United States in simplicity, in definiteness and in relative brevity. Because that Constitution was confined to fundamental principles and all matters of mere legislative detail and procedure were excluded from it, it has existed for a century and a half without any amendment which affects or alters its basic principles of government. The various amendments from the eleventh to the twenty-first, which simply repeals the eighteenth, all deal with matters of procedure within the limits of the principles upon which the Constitution rests. This of itself marks a stupendous achievement by the members of that great convention which was in session at Philadelphia just one hundred and fifty-one years ago.

This fact explains why public opinion in the United States, so often indifferent for long periods of time to really important matters of political and economic policy, bestirs itself almost instantly when it becomes conscious that a basic constitutional principle is at stake. This is the explanation of the uprising, so extraordinary in character and so successful, against adoption of the proposal made to the Congress some eighteen months ago to destroy the independence of the Supreme Court of the United States, that body being one of the three elements of political power into which the Federal Government is divided. The people will resist and punish any attempt to impair the independence of that supreme judicial body, which is the only representative they have in what concerns the present-day interpretation of the underlying principles and practices of their government. The President of the United States, who is the only public officer chosen by the whole people, represents their last expression of opinion, which may have been one based on calm judgment or on heated emotion. The members of the Senate and of the House of Representatives, almost uniformly chosen by a small fraction of the possible voters in their several electorates, respond quickly and with rare exceptions to local or group pressure and interest. Few indeed are the senators and representatives who would hearken to the classic declaration of Edmund Burke that he owed to his constituents not only his voice and his vote, but his conscience and his intelligence. Still smaller is the number of those who would repeat the declaration of Senator Edmunds of Vermont, made on the floor of the Senate, that while a senator is chosen from and by the voters of a state, he becomes, when elected, a senator of the United States, and the whole American people is his constituency.

It is the power of ultimate judicial interpretation of what the Constitution may mean in any given case which has protected that Constitution from disastrous revolution. Were it possible to apply it or amend it, in effect though not in form, through emotional outbursts or under the influence of pressure groups and self-seeking interests, the Government of the United States would have gone on the rocks long ago. The American people may be, as so many commentators think, slow to take an interest in the serious matters of political life, but from the building of this nation to the present day they have never failed to rally to the defense of the cornerstone of their great national edifice.

There are, however, various ways in which the foundations of our American democracy may be undermined subtly and without attracting public notice. One of these ways is by revolution through taxation. The function of taxation in a democratic social and political order is simply to provide ways and means to carry on an efficient and liberal government by requiring the entire citizenship to contribute, each according to his means, toward the support of that government. It is essential that practically every citizen should make some conscious contribution through taxation to the support of the government, no matter how small that contribution may be, in order that he feel a sense of responsibility for what his government does or leaves undone, as well as realize that the money which the government is spending is in part his money and not merely the money of other persons who are better off than himself. It is important that the whole body of citizenship shall be called upon to contribute through taxation in proportion to their ability to do so. But in establishing what this proportion shall be, the ruling principle must be simply the needs of the government well administered, and not any attempt to penalize those citizens of the democratic state who are in more fortunate financial position than their fellows. The moment that the power of taxation is used in an attempt to redistribute the national savings and to penalize as though they were criminals those individuals whose honest accumulations are large, that moment taxation has departed from the principles upon which a democracy rests and has started toward the building of

a collectivist state, by unseen and almost unsuspected
forces.

Moreover, this revolution through taxation goes deep
into the underlying principles of Democracy and does
those principles grave damage. It tends to destroy one
whole great field of public service, indeed the greatest
field of public service, which is that of unofficial undertakings in the fields of charity, of education, of scientific
research, of medicine and public health, in the establishment of libraries and public art galleries, and in a hundred other ways. It has unfortunately become custom-
ary in the United States to speak of institutions of public
service as either public or private; but there are no
private institutions of public service. A private institution is one maintained for profit. If an institution is
established and carried on in any one of the fields named,
then it is an institution for the public service and is public, not private. The distinction is not between public
and private, but between official and unofficial. The
postal system, the maintenance of common schools and
of state universities, of governmental hospitals and
libraries are all forms of official public service, but
there are literally thousands of like institutions of public
service which are unofficial and non-governmental. They
have been established and are maintained by the bene-
factions of private citizens who have gladly given in
this form aid to their fellow men. To tax the property of a university, a church, a hospital or a library so
established and maintained, would be just as unreasona-
ble and as unfair as to tax a post office, a public park or
a governmental hospital. Every form of public service
in a democratic state is to be encouraged and invited; it

should never be made more difficult or lessened in amount or in extent. It is in this field in particular that a democracy must teach the government to mind its own proper business.

A second method of weakening the principles upon which Democracy rests, without amending the Constitution, has been found in the habit which has been steadily growing at Washington and at several of the state capitals for a generation past. This is to set up administrative boards or commissions in a great variety of fields and then to attempt by legislation to give them authority practically to control the administration of the major portion of the people's business. Nothing could be more anti-democratic than that and nothing more adverse to the public welfare. It is the fixed habit of these commissions and administrative boards, whether federal or state, steadily to increase the area of their attempted jurisdiction and with more and more particularity to specify and direct the form of business activities of almost every kind. Just now an attempt is making to extend this revolutionary habit in a score of ways, each one of which represents an expression of the ambition of the busybody and the uplifter, with no concern for what Democracy means or for how it can be made to work. Many of those who are engaged in these governmental activities are fearful lest the totalitarian state, whether Communist or Fascist, find a foothold in the United States, and yet that which they are doing day by day is to imitate the totalitarian state in the field which has particularly aroused their personal interest and activity.

The unfortunate fact relative to these unseen but persistent underminings of the democratic principle is that they go forward so largely without any cognizance on the part of the general public. If this condition is permitted to continue, the day will come when American public opinion will awake to find that its form of government has been changed, that its democracy has been destroyed, and yet that its Constitution has not been amended.

All this is largely due to the fact that it has become an American habit, whenever any disaster occurs or any new problem presents itself, not to insist upon higher intelligence or better morals, but to pass a law. We may well go back to the New York State Convention which met one hundred and fifty years ago at Poughkeepsie to ratify the Federal Constitution, then pending, and listen to these words which Alexander Hamilton spoke to his associates in that epoch-marking body: "All governments, even the most despotic, depend, in a great degree, on opinion. . . . It is the fortunate situation of our country, that the minds of the people are exceedingly enlightened and refined. Here, then, we may expect the laws to be proportionately agreeable to the standard of a perfect policy, and the wisdom of public measures to consist with the most intimate conformity between the views of the representative and his constituent."

It remains to mention one other anti-democratic tendency in our government which from the time of George Washington has been felt by many to be a real danger to the democratic republic. That is the exaltation of the power of the presidential office. There was much discussion of this question in the Constitutional Convention of 1787 itself, and it has not failed to attract public attention from that day to this. It is plain on the one hand that the presidential office must have dignity and authority proportionate to its distinction and that in the field of administration it should be supreme if it is to be effective. It is when the direct power of the executive is extended beyond the field of administration to that of policy-making and policy-shaping, which are solely the function of the legislative branch of the government, that it may easily become a danger to Democracy.

Washington himself, keenly alive to the criticisms which were directed at the presidential office, was very reluctant to accept election to a second term as president and flatly refused to consider election for a third term. That question was never raised again except in theory until there was a well-organized movement within the Republican party to nominate President Grant for a third term in 1876.

Thirty-one different men have held the office of President of the United States. Of these eleven were elected to serve a second term, one—Cleveland—after an interval of four years. Fourteen Presidents were elected for one term only. Six succeeded to the presidency from the vice-presidential office, and of these two, Theodore Roosevelt and Coolidge, were subsequently elected to the presidency.

The question was raised both in the case of Theodore Roosevelt and in that of Coolidge, whether candidacy for another election to the presidency would under the circumstances involve the principle of a third presidential term. In each case the matter was resolved by the action of the two presidents themselves. In 1912, however, four years after his second presidential term had expired, Theodore Roosevelt felt that political conditions were such as to justify him in undertaking another candidacy for the presidential office. That candidacy resulted in defeat.

When the question of the possibility of a third presidential term is raised, this is invariably done by individuals and groups which feel that their own continuance in posts of authority and influence is dependent upon the personality of the president who put them in those posts. No president has himself ever sought election to a third term, unless the exceptional circumstances in the case of Theodore Roosevelt are to be so interpreted. The most powerful and the most highly organized movement for a third term was that on behalf of President Grant. Although this movement failed in 1876, it was renewed with the utmost vigor in 1880, and held the work of the Republican National Convention of that year in check for several days before it was finally overcome.

The well-considered public opinion of the nation in respect to a third presidential term cannot be better expressed than in the words of the resolution adopted by the House of Representatives on December 15, 1875. The text of that resolution was as follows:

RESOLVED—That, in the opinion of this House, the precedent established by Washington and other Presidents of the United States, in retiring from the presidential office after their second term, has become, by universal concurrence, a part of our republican system of government, and that any departure from this time-honored custom would be unwise, unpatriotic, and fraught with peril to our free institutions.

This resolution was adopted by a vote of 233 in the

affirmative to 18 in the negative, with 38 absent and not voting. Of those voting for this resolution 158 were Democrats, 73 were Republicans and 2 were Independents. Of the 18 negative votes all were cast by Republicans, presumably supporters of the movement to elect President Grant for a third term.

To all intents and purposes the language of this very clear and important resolution has become the expression of a national policy which must be looked upon as fundamental. It has amended the Constitution in fact although not in form. No president is at all likely himself to propose its reversal or modification, but on the other hand no president can always control the unwise and injudicious activities of some of those who wish to be known to the public as his friends.

These three practices and policies—revolution by taxation, increasing control by bureaucracy of the life and occupations of the population, and that change in the authority of the presidential office which would in effect give to the president legislative as well as executive power—are the outstanding dangers to which our American democracy is exposed from within. It is quite conceivable that the democratic republic might be more completely and more quickly broken down and demoralized through the growth of the power of these policies than by outward and visible attack from the totalitarian states themselves. New evidence of this possibility is to be found in the fact that the principal and most obvious result of the endeavors now making throughout the world to cope with the unprecedented economic depression is to increase the difficulties of each and every country by reason of the policies of economic nationalism which those countries have, almost without exception, undertaken. This fact of itself constitutes a new danger to Democracy. The certain result of a continuance of these policies will be still farther to weaken and to endanger our own democratic republic.

It is eighty years since Macaulay wrote his now famous and much-quoted letter relative to what he believed to be the inevitable breakdown of the American democracy in the not distant future. His analysis of moving forces and their probable effects was most acute, but he overlooked a fundamental fact of commanding importance. That fact is that in the United States the social and political order does not rest upon or involve any permanent division of the population into fixed economic and social classes. In Europe, since the time of the feudal system, such a distinction, with a long historical background behind it, has existed almost everywhere and is only now breaking down slowly and with difficulty. It is the absence in the United States of any such group of fixed and definite social and economic distinctions as Macaulay assumed which deprives his argument and his prophecy of the force which would otherwise attach to them.

Convinced believers in Democracy have its future in their own hands. Its protection can be found, and found only, in an intelligent, alert and courageous public opinion, armed for action with that vision without which the people perish.

IX

WAIT AND SEE

An address delivered at the opening of the
twenty-sixth season of the
Institute of Arts and Sciences, Columbia University,
McMillin Academic Theatre, New York,
October 17, 1938

WAIT AND SEE

Mr. Director and our Friends of the Institute: At the opening of the twenty-sixth year of this organized branch of our University's work, we find ourselves, we must find ourselves, dazed and confused by the happenings in the world in which we live.

We have the good fortune, particularly those of us who live in the United States, to have most admirable and accurate and prompt sources of information. No matter how distant any great happening may be, we have accurate knowledge concerning it as rapidly as the electric spark can bring it to us. American journalism has never in all its history shown itself so excellent as it has during the past six months. The promptness, the fullness, the definiteness and the fairness of the information which we have had, particularly through the highly skilled representatives of *The New York Times* and of the *New York Herald Tribune*, of the Associated Press and of the United Press, have put the American people in position to know very much about vitally important happenings elsewhere which were known only partially, if at all, to the inhabitants of the countries where they were taking place.

I am in position to assure you that ordinarily well-informed men and women in European countries have, during the past six months, waited for the arrival of the American newspapers in order that they might get their first full and accurate information of what was going on

in their own lands and on the part of their own governments.

Of course, one reason for that is the policy which has
everywhere been adopted in Europe of controlling the
press, either by influence and persuasion or by direct
dominance and compulsion. You would be quite sur-
prised to know that great speeches have been delivered
by members of governments in other lands which were
printed verbatim in a New York paper and yet were
referred to in only the most casual fashion in the newspapers of the land to which the speaker belonged.

We Americans are beginning to pay the penalty and
to reap the advantage of our century and a half of history. We have been able, under our Constitution and
the form of political, social, and economic liberty which
it set up and protected, to build up a nation which contradicts all the fundamental principles upon which the
present-day totalitarian states rest their case. We have
shown ourselves able to take fundamental institutions
and ideals, primarily of English origin, then shared by
French and Dutch and Scandinavians, and to make them
deep enough, wide enough, strong enough, to support
and to maintain a nation to which any well-meaning and
honest person, of whatever tongue, from whatever land,
might come, to begin the task of making his own way
under the protection of American principles and American ideals.

Most of those persons have come to us as individuals
or in small groups, but on two or three important occa-
sions, they came to us in very considerable number and
for specific reasons. After the potato famine in Ireland
nearly a hundred years ago, a great Irish immigration

began, which brought to us a body of men and women who have played an extraordinary part in the life of the American people from that day to this. They have been in public life, they have been in our social and economic organization, they have been in our family life, and they have made a place for themselves which has led us to hold them in gratitude and high respect. After the failure of the German revolution of 1848, there came to us an extraordinary stream of Germans, men and women of the highest type, who settled in small part in New York, more largely in Milwaukee and Cincinnati and St. Louis and in the State of Nebraska, and quickly became a very powerful element in American life. Out yonder, on Morningside Heights, is a statue of Carl Schurz, who was one of the great names, perhaps the greatest name, in that movement, a general in the Union Army under Lincoln, a United States Senator, a member of the Cabinet, editor of an important newspaper and a personality of outstanding importance.

In like fashion we have had a great stream of Italians, a smaller stream of French, who are not so given to migration as the other European people, and we have had a very remarkable influx of Jewish people from every part of Europe, including particularly Germany and Central and Eastern Europe. They have come to play a very influential part in our intellectual and business and political life.

Now what would happen if we Americans were to apply to our population some of the controlling principles of a totalitarian state? Suppose we began by expelling all those who were not originally American. Who were originally American? The very small num-

ber, some three and one half millions, who constituted
the population of these thirteen sovereign states, so-
called, a hundred and fifty years ago? Everybody else
would have to be examined, repressed, made to conform
to type or be expelled. Our three and one half million,
if they could discover themselves and their children and
grandchildren, would have a very difficult problem before them.

Why is it that the people of the United States have
been able to deal with this question of multifarious races
and languages and nationalities? Why is it that the
British people have been able to do it? And why is it
that it seems so difficult, so impossible and so distasteful
to the believers in the present-day totalitarian state?
That is not an easy question to answer, because the totalitarian state contradicts in every one of its underlying
principles, in all of its arguments and in each one of its
ideals, all the practical conditions of twentieth-century
life in this world of ours. While our various nationalities
and governments have been going their respective ways,
unseen, unmeasured and almost unknown forces have
been altering the world in every essential particular.
The electric spark destroyed the old world and created
a new one. It made the happenings in Sydney, in Canton, in Tokyo, and in Moscow, just as quickly known to
us as happenings in Boston and Chicago and St. Louis.
It made it possible for ideas to go round the world faster
than the most rapid of airplanes. It made it possible for
arguments and principles to exert themselves and to
produce results almost in an instant. You turn on your
radio and you listen to a voice from Moscow, from
Berlin, from Rome, from Paris, from London, from

Chicago, from San Francisco, as if it were the voice of your nearest neighbor.

We have long ago gained the full results of the voyage of Columbus. There are no more worlds left for us to discover and we have found, to our great surprise, that if one knows how to do it, he may go round this present world in three days and a half. It is not so long ago that Jules Verne wrote his extraordinary book, *Around the World in Eighty Days,* and it was thought to be a dream which might some day perhaps be achieved in actuality. We have seen this journey made in three days and a half, and no one dares say that sooner or later it will not be made between daylight and dawn.

We have put all the resources of each and every part of the earth at the disposal of every other part which wishes it and can pay for it. One need no longer be deprived of the excellent and valuable products of the tropics because he lives in the North Temperate Zone or in the Arctic Zone, and similarly the dweller in the tropics may have with great speed those articles which are grown and produced in this part of the world and still farther north. The result is, while we do not seem to realize it and our governments do not seem to understand it in the least, that mankind has been intertwined in a most amazing fashion. If today we were to try to dissect this world of ideas, of political happenings, of economic forces and of industrial achievements and turn each element back to where it started and keep it there, this world would pass out of existence in an early death through suffocation and starvation. In other words, the world is one. The various parts of the world are wholly interdependent.

We are very proud of our leadership in various branches of industry. We have in this country some twenty-five million or some twenty-six million automobiles. Not one single one of them could be built and equipped in this country alone. That example might be multiplied a thousand times. The world needs for the most ordinary and the most obvious articles of daily life products from some distant and remote lands that were quite inaccessible fifty years, seventy-five years or a hundred years ago.

What is the lesson from all this? The lesson is that in our political and economic life we are two generations behind the facts, and our problems, our sufferings, our sorrows, our dangers, our anxieties, are due to the fact, I repeat, that in our economic and political life we are at least two generations behind the times. In other words, we are nominally living in a world which does not exist and we are refusing to live in the world which lies open before us. It is a most extraordinary phenomenon, and the historian five hundred years hence will have some very interesting things to say about the times in which we live, for never before in the history of mankind has there been any such gap between actual human relationships and the facts, or apparent facts, of economic and political life as they exist today.

The consequence is that each nation, considering itself in seventeenth- and eighteenth-century terms that have been long since outgrown, considering itself a wholly independent and sovereign nation, says to the rest of the world, "I must do just what I please; I must take care of myself alone; I will take an academic interest in other people, if you please, and if I am a Christian, I will probably consent to pray for them occasionally. But I will not do anything that contradicts my conception of myself and my people as a wholly independent and self-centered unit in human life." That is the problem which confronts us today.

The alternative before the people of this day and generation, and I say this with all seriousness, is either to solve that problem constructively or to see our western civilization decay and die.

Civilizations have died before. We now spend a very considerable time in digging up the physical evidences of their existence and achievements and remains, and we are constantly astonished at what they were able to do centuries ago, in Egypt, in Mesopotamia, in the far Orient. We have seen the great Roman Empire, after its magnificent history of hundreds of years, break and go to pieces, and we have seen a reconstruction of the western world which took nearly a thousand years for its accomplishment; and some of the great achievements of that old world of Greece and Rome, in philosophy, in literature, in the drama and in the fine arts, have never yet been equaled or surpassed. In other words, there can be no certainty that civilization will continue to develop constructively and broadly and healthfully because we have these great lessons of the past staring us in the face.

This is the year 1938 of the Christian era. We have been listening and our ancestors have been listening, apparently with sympathetic understanding, to eloquent appeals for a life of faith, of reasonableness, of charity, of human kindliness, and in this year 1938 not only are there brutal and cruel wars going forward, undeclared and thereby avoiding the responsibilities which attach through international law to a combatant, not only have we that, but we have every nation in the world arming for what it calls "defense," spending thousands of millions of that wealth which is so sorely needed for the satisfaction and relief of the great masses of the world's populations. There are literally tens of millions of people waiting for some opportunity to have life made more comfortable, more safe, more abundant in opportunity, and here we are, all of us, without exception, wringing the money from our taxpayers to arm ourselves for defense. Every government of the world is preaching peace and those who are most likely to make war are preaching it most fervently.

What is the explanation of these amazing contradictions? What has happened in this twentieth-century world to bring about a situation of this kind? It is only twenty years ago next month that we all shouted with acclaim because an armistice was signed at the end of a great war, which made the world safe for democracy, and democracy has never been in such danger as it is today, twenty years after that event. What is it that has happened?

In a private interview which I had last summer with one of the most distinguished statesmen of Europe, he made an amazing statement upon which I have reflected a great deal from that day to this. He said, "Doctor Butler, practically all the people of every nation on earth want peace and good relations with every other people, but about twelve or fifteen hundred human beings are making all the trouble for this world and putting its institutions in gravest danger."

Why can we not do something about it? That is the question, my friends; not only why can we not do something about it, but why do we not do something about it? You could not get any congregation or convention of intelligent men and women in any land, least of all in this land, to pass a resolution in favor of war. In fact, it is not ten years since sixty-three nations formally signed a renunciation of war as an instrument of national policy, and then went on arming more rapidly than ever. What is the explanation?

My answer to that question is an absolute breakdown of morality in all that affects international obligations and international relations; a lack of any sense of responsibility toward the present and the future generations of men in connection with the great commitments which have been made in our time. There is a gap between profession and practice which can be bridged only by a sense of moral support which will lead governments, compel governments, to carry out their obligations made in solemn treaties, and to respond to the highest ideals of the aspirations of their several peoples.

As conditions have developed, the American people have been put in a position of great responsibility. There is a notion, sedulously cultivated by certain politicians and by certain portions of the press, that the United States has always been isolated from the rest of the world. There is not one scintilla of truth in that statement. It has been just the opposite. From the very beginning of our history, we have eagerly sought to intertwine ourselves, our institutions, our ideals and our policies, with the older nations of Europe.

We began with Benjamin Franklin, who spent nearly twenty-five years telling the people of Great Britain and of France what we were doing, what we were trying to do, why we believed in it all. It was Thomas Jefferson who spent years in France, and, as a matter of dramatic fact, sat in the gallery at Versailles, in the hall in which the convention was held which passed the Declaration of the Rights of Man thirteen years after the adoption of his own Declaration of Independence. John Adams, our second President, living in London, wrote for the English people explanations of our new Constitution; what it was, what its principles were, and why we thought it would commend itself to sympathetic attention of the European countries.

And from that date on, through our great Secretaries of State—John Quincy Adams, Daniel Webster, Hamilton Fish, John Hay, Elihu Root—we have been giving counsel and co-operation to every great advancing movement in Europe, Asia or Africa.

The reason we are isolated, or said to be isolated, appears to rest upon two sentences which have been misquoted so many, many times for so many, many years. We are told that George Washington warned us against entangling alliances. Nobody has proposed an entangling alliance and Washington never said anything of the kind. The phrase, "entangling alliances," was used by Thomas Jefferson in his first inaugural and it had specific reference to the Napoleonic Wars which were then going on. We had rebelled against British domination and we were rebuilding relations with the British people. The French had been our allies and helpers. They had passed over into Napoleonic despotism. The wars that were going on naturally invited our participation. Jefferson warned us against them. **But** it so happened, without any very great skill, that **we** managed to get in the War of 1812.

The present situation began in a constructive fashion just forty years ago, and the United States, from 1898 to the Great War, was active in leadership in trying to solve these problems of which I speak, through building up an organized society of nations. We did not wait for anybody else; we took the lead, and we proposed such action.

In August, 1898, one of the most remarkable papers in all history was made public. It was an invitation issued in the name of the Czar of All the Russias, by Count Mouraviev, his Foreign Minister, to the nations of the world to meet and take counsel together as to how to ensure prosperity and peace through international co-operation. One of the very first acceptances of that invitation came from the government of the United States. President McKinley was deeply touched by it and he appointed a very remarkable delegation to represent us. At its head was Andrew D. White, President of Cornell University and a most distinguished statesman of large international experience. Associated with him was President Seth Low of Columbia University; our Minister to the Netherlands, Mr. Stanford Newel; Captain Mahan, afterward the famous Admiral Mahan; a distinguished army officer, Captain William Crozier; and Mr. Frederick W. Holls, a most distinguished alumnus of this university, whose early death deprived the world of a very great service toward international activity and progress. That great conference met at The

Hague in 1899. From the standpoint of the call issued by the Czar of All the Russias, it was a failure.

But it was saved from total collapse by the American delegation. They proposed, if nothing else were done, that a permanent court of arbitration should be established.

If you will read the instructions of Elihu Root, given to our representatives at the International Conference of 1908, you will find the finest exhibition of American principles and policy that has ever been penned by any one. That conference made some advance, producing a court of justice in addition to the existing court of arbitration.

At that time public opinion in the United States was very alert, very acute and very anxious for something to happen, and this is what happened, although I fancy that no one who reads these words remembers that it did happen. It is the most outstanding act of vision and constructive policy in relation to foreign affairs in the history of the American people. This resolution, let me say again, was introduced into the House of Representatives in the month of June, 1910, reported from the Committee on Foreign Affairs unanimously, reading as follows:

RESOLVED—That a commission of five members be appointed by the President of the United States to consider the expediency of utilizing existing international agencies for the purpose of limiting the armaments of the nations of the world by international agreement, and of constituting the combined navies of the world an international force for the preservation of universal peace, and to consider and report upon any other means to diminish the expenditures of government for military purposes and to lessen the probabilities of war.

What happened to that remarkable resolution, a resolution of vision, a resolution of highest principle? It was adopted by the House of Representatives by unanimous vote. It was sent to the Senate of the United States, reported by the Committee on Foreign Relations, and adopted by the Senate by unanimous vote. Both Houses of the Congress of the United States, Republicans and Democrats alike, twenty-nine years ago called upon the United States Government to lead and to establish an international police force for the protection of the peace of the world!

How many Americans of 1938 realize where public opinion was in 1910? What happened? President Taft signed the resolution very gladly. He then asked two of his friends—I suppose I may speak of this now—to go to Europe and inquire unofficially and informally what the answer would be to such an invitation if he were to issue it. For obvious reasons he did not approach those governments through the ordinary diplomatic channels. He wanted informally and personally to sound them out. The two friends whom he asked to make the inquiry were Mr. Elihu Root and myself. I went to London and consulted Sir Edward Grey, then Foreign Minister in the British Government. I went to Paris and consulted Monsieur Philippe Berthelot, the permanent and very distinguished and efficient head of the Foreign Office. I went to Germany and consulted Chancellor von Bülow and the Kaiser himself. I went to Austria and consulted the Foreign Office in Vienna. Mr. Root went to The Hague, to Paris and to London, and consulted leaders in the governments of their countries. We both reported to Mr. Taft that the reception of the proposal was very polite, but "Wait and See; not yet, Wait and See." They waited and they saw.

It was only four years before the calamity came and the world had those appalling years which we used to think could at least be described as the last of their kind. Finally the world had paid the bill, so we thought.

Mr. Thomas J. Watson, a Trustee of Columbia University and one of our most distinguished men of affairs, has recently shown us what could have been done in this country alone by the cost of that war to us, and it is worth recalling some of the outstanding items. The cost of war to us was nearly fifty-one billion dollars, and we were in it only a year and a half. Mr. Watson has shown that that would have provided the wiring for electricity for nine million, four hundred thousand urban and rural homes now without current; that it would have paid off every farm mortgage in the United States; that it would have equipped with bathrooms the five million, seven hundred and fifty thousand farms without them; that it would have added to the endowments for education now in existence, $1,500,000,000; that it would have built four consolidated schools at a cost of a quarter of a million each in every county in the United States; that it would have constructed airports to the amount of one million dollars in every county in the United States; that it would have provided for the prevention of floods and soil erosion, five billion dollars; that it would have established a trust fund which, at 3 per cent, would provide $100 a month in pension for every blind person and deaf-mute in the United States; that it would have built ten bridges, each equivalent to the Triborough Bridge; that it would have built

another canal across Panama at the cost of the present
one; that it would duplicate the recovery and relief program of the United States from 1932 to 1938; that, we
spent while waiting and seeing.

My friends, the practical lesson which I draw from
all this is that if we insist upon the policy of "Wait and
See" and if the democracies of the world persist in that
policy, all this will happen again, and this time it will
not make the world safe for democracy, but it will make
the world safe for a long period of darkness and despair.

What the government of the United States and the
people of the United States have now opportunity to do
is to take their stand on that great resolution of 1910,
adopted unanimously by both Houses of the Congress,
without regard to party, and say to the world, "We have
waited and seen long enough. Come now and sit down
with us in the terms of this appeal and bring about a
reconstruction of the society of nations that will give
opportunity for us to put an end to this armed fear and
despair and get started again on the path that we were
on from 1898 to 1910."

No other people can do it. They have all created
their antagonisms and their frictions. If it is going to
be done at all, it is going to be the service and the leadership of the American people to the world of today and
tomorrow.

Three weeks ago when the European situation was at
its worst, so tense that no one knew what might happen
any moment, the appeal of the President of the United
States to the heads of those governments to settle their
differences without war made an impression on Europe
which was perfectly marvellous. Unless you have been

in position to see the reaction to that appeal by the different groups and classes and the various European countries, you have no notion of the influence which it exerted. People said everywhere, "The government of the United States must be speaking the spirit and opinion of the American people in calling us all to keep our word, to make sure that we have renounced war as an instrument of national policy and to settle these differences by discussion and by arbitration."

It may be said they were not settled in a satisfactory fashion; they were settled in ways that are open to great criticism. Nevertheless, the appalling catastrophe upon the innocent, the old, the young, the ill, the infirm, the appalling catastrophe which present-day war would mean was averted for at least a time. We in America have no conception of what was going on in England. We have no conception of the way in which they were compelled or felt compelled to dig in their great parks for opportunities to go underground to escape the bomb and the poison gas; children going through the streets each carrying his protective gas mask; women all having their instructions as to what they were to do; and on September 28 every railway station crowded to capacity with old and young trying to get to Scotland, to Wales, to the west of England, where it was thought the invading hosts would not be able to drop bombs or gas from airplanes.

That, my friends, is 1938, twenty years after Armistice Day. I repeat, the one dangerous policy today is Wait and See. It is the popular policy with government because they are almost without exception cowardly. They are waiting for pressure, and most of the pressure which they get comes from small, organized minorities, self-seeking in some respect. But that great appeal which ought to come from the people as a whole, without any self-interest, caring simply for principle, for morality, for their fellow men, that appeal to governments is lacking and therefore governments Wait and See. Believe me, it they insist upon the policy of Wait and See, there will be plenty to be seen in your lifetime and mine.

X

THE FAMILY OF NATIONS, 1938

An address with world-wide broadcast delivered over the
Columbia Broadcasting Network, New York, Armistice Day,
November 11, 1938
with addresses by the Rt. Hon. David Lloyd George, former
Prime Minister of Great Britain; M. Henry-Haye, Mayor of
Versailles, France; Doctor Bo Östen Undén, former Minister
of Foreign Affairs of Sweden; Doctor Paul van Zeeland, for-
mer Prime Minister of Belgium; Major General John F.
O'Ryan (United States Army, retired).

THE FAMILY OF NATIONS
1938

Let us look facts in the face. Twenty years ago this day armed hostilities were ended in the most disastrous war which the world had ever seen. The cost in human life and in human savings had been stupendous, and the victory was hailed as making the world safe for democracy and opening the path to permanent peace. On this twentieth anniversary of that Armistice, democracy, instead of being safe, is in greater danger than it has ever been, and the path to permanent peace is, for the time being at least, blocked by ignorance, by selfishness, by abandonment of moral standards in international relations and by governmental thirst for expansion and for power. The people are everywhere eager for peace, but their governments, while proclaiming peace, with equal eagerness are preparing for war in unprecedented fashion.

Those four years of devastating war and their appalling losses were all in vain. History does not record any more convincing evidence of the futility of war. The nations which were associated together as victors are now seen to have lost everything for which they fought and made such stupendous sacrifice, while those who, as aggressors and in violation of treaties, by the invasion of Belgium commenced hostilities and were after four years defeated, are now seen to have won everything for which they then contended and much more.

In interpreting the significance of happenings in the history of man, it is quite futile to keep repeating the question If. If this had been done or If that had been left undone, conditions and circumstances would today be wholly different. While all this may be perfectly true, it is none the less without meaning or significance in dealing with the stern facts of the moment.

The sternest of these stern facts is that public morality has pretty completely disappeared from the field of international relations. Treaties and other governmental obligations are seen to mean nothing, and it is futile for governments to continue to make treaties with one another until the rule of morals is re-established. "He that sweareth to his own hurt, and changeth not" is no longer found in the field of international policy and international relations.

A way has now been found by which war may be undertaken, as in Spain, in Ethiopia, and in China, without any declaration of war and with utter contempt for treaties and for the rules and principles of international law. The rule of blind and self-seeking force has for the time being established itself in control of human affairs. What can be done about it?

There are those who would accept conditions and circumstances of this sort, yield to control by them and, as they would say, continue to hope for the best. That is sheer, blind fatalism and does not rise to the plane of either intelligence or morality. On the other hand, there are the attitude and outlook of those who refuse to surrender to hopeless discouragement and who, as they look back over the history of western civilization, find the present to be but one more of those tragic reactions which for three thousand years have marked human progress in this western world. It is to this viewpoint, and to this alone, that the future belongs. We are most certainly surrounded by darkness, both moral and intellectual, but let us look upon it as a darkness which precedes the dawn. It must be our unflagging effort to have the sun rise again, and that without too long delay.

The fates have put the future of the world for the next century or more in the hands of the American people. These tragic happenings and these problems which are so glibly referred to as European or Asiatic, and thereby far removed from us, are nothing of the sort. They are American in every sense of the word because they are world-wide and fundamental and, above all, moral. The American people are by far the best organized politically and by far the most powerful morally in the whole world. All that is needed is for the American people to recognize those facts and to rise to the height of their opportunity for self-improvement and leadership.

In the early part of the year 1919, the public opinion of the American people was practically unanimous in favor of assuming that leadership through taking part in the organization of a society of nations and to build, through conference and consultation and without appeal to force, a new world of prosperity and established peace. A change of nine votes in the Senate of the United States when the Treaty of Versailles was under consideration would have ratified that treaty on the part of the American government and so established our leadership in world organization. There was a large majority of the Senate for ratification, but not the two-thirds vote required by the Constitution. Had ratification taken place, the means would then have been provided for the peaceful and orderly solution, under American influence, of those problems which have just now led once more to rule by force and threat of force instead of by reasonable conference and consultation. Later on, a change of five votes in the Senate of the United States would have brought the Government of the United States to the support of the Permanent Court of International Justice, which our own statesmen had suggested and powerfully aided to bring into existence. Again a large majority of the Senate voted for ratification, but again, the necessary two-thirds vote not having been reached, a small minority defeated the express will of the American people. Had ratification taken place, there would have been established the practice of appealing to judicial process and to judicial impartiality for the settlement of those thousand and one international questions which so constantly arise, bringing possible ill feeling and antagonism in their train.

If the two American political parties, particularly that one which was successful in the presidential election of 1920, had remained true to their pledges given to the American people, this world would have been a different place. The Republican National Platform of 1920 clearly and definitely committed that party to agreement among the nations to preserve the peace of the world, and without the powerful address in support of that policy which President Harding delivered at Marion, Ohio, on August 28, 1920, he could not have been chosen President of the United States. It is for the American people to reflect upon their own very large share of re-

sponsibility for what has happened throughout the world
to make either national prosperity or international peace
almost impossible.

There is no time to be lost. Our truly great American people must become conscious of their moral responsibility to their fellow men and see to it that their
government, which has had as its spokesmen such magnificent personalities as Washington and Hamilton, Jefferson and Madison, Webster and Clay, Seward and
Hamilton Fish and Root, be not lacking in leadership
and moral power at this tragic and fateful hour.

It is with the greatest pleasure that I now present
to this world-wide audience a veteran statesman of
long years of service to whom the cause of international
peace is most precious. As a member of the British Government from 1905 to 1922 and either Chancellor of
the Exchequer or Prime Minister during the years of
the Great War and for four years thereafter, Mr.
Lloyd George has had the most intimate association
with the facts and tendencies which have made and are
making the history of civilization. I present to you the
Right Honorable David Lloyd George. We take you
now to London, England—

MR. LLOYD GEORGE: My friends in the great and
free continent of America—

I do not recollect a period during my lifetime when
the international atmosphere was more charged with
distrust, antagonism and apprehension. The Pact of
Munich which it was hoped by its authors would bring
peace in our lifetime has been followed everywhere by

feverish appeals and new projects for increasing the weapons of war and for strengthening defenses against murderous attacks on land and sea. There are sanguinary wars now being waged in three continents—one in Asia, another in Europe and a third in Africa. Each of these desperate conflicts is spreading desolation, terror and death amongst millions of harmless civilians. The war which has been and still is ravaging Ethiopia is overlooked in the more spectacular wars which are desolating China and Spain. Nevertheless, the emphasis in every country is not upon the best means of securing universal pacification, but upon the quickest methods of producing the largest output of machinery and the training of the largest number of men to wage effective war. That constitutes the most alarming feature of the world situation today. Unless measures are taken and taken boldly and taken promptly by the rulers of nations to secure a better understanding and a saner temper, a clash is inevitable on a scale which will rock civilization to its foundations and precipitate a catastrophe which will bury the work of centuries amongst the ruins.

The thrill of relief which passed through Europe when it was known that a temporary peace had been patched up over the Czechoslovakia dispute shows how deep and general is the horror of war amongst all classes. When gas masks were distributed at every door to save the dwellers inside from being strangled by poison gas, when men were working overtime to tear up the beautiful parks of London into trenches to shield its inhabitants from bombs which were expected within twenty-four hours to rain destruction from the skies above, one can realize how welcome was the news that the government had negotiated a respite from the impending horror. In that hour of escape there was no disposition to examine the terms which had been exacted by the dictators from affrighted democracies.

The panic is now subsiding, and reflection is beginning. It is noticeable that the first reaction is a universal demand for stronger defenses. The mind of nations without distinction of race or of party is concentrated on that problem. It seems as if the people of Europe despaired of any attempt to negotiate a general world peace and brotherhood. The failure of the League of Nations has disheartened the advocates of universal peace. In France and Britain there is much talk in official circles of negotiating pacts to propitiate the dictators. That might effect a postponement of an ultimate conflict, but the interval would be filled with the clangor of war preparations and there would be only an arming peace which would paralyze industry, cripple social amelioration and shatter the nerve of civilization.

To secure permanent peace, a world pacification is essential. Without it we shall breathe daily an atmosphere of war. France and Britain cannot disarm unless Germany and Italy disarm. Germany cannot afford to lay down her arms unless Russia reduces her armaments. Russia cannot reduce her armed forces as long as Japan has a powerful army and a frightening one. Japan cannot even discuss disarmament as long as there is war in China. America must go on building up her navy and air force as long as Japan is increasing her armaments by sea, land and air. Two- or even four-power pacts to divert the activities of the military dictators temporarily from Britain and France will not give the world peace.

It will disembarrass the aggressor states of all danger of interference from the western democracies whilst they are pursuing their designs in other directions. Their access to the east has already been cleared by the removal of the Czechoslovakian Republic from the road. The only chance of a world peace is an assembly of nations to discuss without reference to past experiments or present ideologies the best means of a just and durable world peace. Where is the statesman who will take this project in hand and will and can press it through? His name will endure forever as one of the greatest benefactors of mankind.

ANNOUNCER: We return you now to America—

DOCTOR BUTLER: We shall now have the pleasure of hearing a voice from France. It is that of M. Henry-Haye, Mayor of Versailles. M. Haye has had a distinguished career in the public service and in the military service of his country. He has visited the United States in years past and knows well some of our western and southern states. He was formerly a member of the Foreign Affairs Committee of the Chamber of Deputies in the French Parliament and is now a member of the Foreign Affairs Committee of the Senate of France. We take you now to Paris, France—

M. HAYE: As an infantryman I fought the last war, first, with the French Colonial troops coming from North Africa. In 1917, the privilege was given to me to be attached to the American Army from the very first day of its entry into the great struggle. I knew then the reactions of men coming from a long distance to participate in the terrific battles in which the Europeans exterminated the best of their youth. This is perhaps the reason why Doctor Nicholas Murray Butler bestowed upon me the honor to speak on this twentieth anniversary of the Armistice to the great American people.

Formerly a deputy, now a member of the Foreign Committee of the French Senate, my public action has always been directed by the main idea of preserving peace. Why is it that peace, which is so much desired by all peoples of the world, is so difficult to maintain? The principal difficulty, as it appears to me, is that the leaders of the nations of the world, instead of acting with the vision of the interests of humankind, have, on the contrary, the general tendency of seeking solutions inspired exclusively by selfish considerations.

As Mayor of Versailles, I know of course the objections raised against the treaty of 1919, signed in my city. It has been said that this treaty was written from a short-sighted viewpoint, neglecting the future of the great European community. Some people claim that selfish motives dictated the action of the negotiators, but it is generally forgotten how difficult their task was. They had to establish drastic measures to prevent new conflicts. They had also to make the demonstration that war could not be declared, and furthermore lost, without costly consequences. It was not easy to find the way to justice after four years of hate, but since 1918 we have had many proofs of our inability to be severe, because we did not know how to be just twenty years ago.

The great democracies do not deny the right to other peoples to choose their régime and to live according to their beliefs and their activities. On the other hand, the democracies consider it their duty to defend their rights and their ideals, not only that of preserving peace, but they have to stand together if they wish to save their liberty. It goes without saying that, in order to have their decisions respected by others, the democratic nations must be strong in discipline but generous too. The fact that this principle has not always been kept in mind by all the leaders of democratic governments explains why the dictators have had such an easy task in realizing their desires. If we were organized, their attitude would be totally different. The only way to reject unjustified claims, the only possibility to check criminal temptations, resides in our own forces.

Doctor Nicholas Murray Butler has written that peace considered only as an ideal does not mean anything if this ideal is not based on reality. With a deep feeling of human solidarity, President Roosevelt called recently on the European leaders to organize a real peace conference with the object of establishing the facts on a solid basis for a collaboration between great and small civilized nations. Let us hope that the day of such a conference will come, but the democracies have got to prepare themselves for such a discussion. If their governments do not get together beforehand to fix in full accord and co-operation conditions of peace, such a meeting would be more dangerous than useful. We must get to work rapidly and steadily. Banishing selfish considerations, there is no doubt that men of good will and will power can achieve success in this task.

Versailles, where world history has been written during the past centuries, is ready to welcome such negotiators, bringing to the world by their plans a real peace. Considering the horrible disaster in which all nations would have been involved by the war that we have avoided by such a narrow margin a few weeks ago, this is the cordial and hopeful message I am glad to convey to the great and generous American people on this twentieth anniversary of the glorious Armistice of 1918, which was concluded thanks to the powerful help of the gallant soldiers of the United States.

ANNOUNCER: We return you now to America—

DOCTOR BUTLER: The Scandinavian peoples have won the confidence and respect of the world by their steadiness of purpose, their clearness of thought and their devotion to the cause of international conference and co-operation. We now have the honor of hearing the voice of an outstanding Swedish jurist who has made his reputation as a member of the government of Sweden, first as Minister without Portfolio, then as Minister of Justice, and then as Minister of Foreign Affairs; who has represented Sweden on the Council of the League of Nations and as delegate to the League of Nations Assembly for many years. There is no voice which can speak for the government of the people of Sweden with more confidence than that of Bo Östen Undén, a member of the Comité du Centre Européen of the Carnegie Endowment for International Peace. We take you now to Stockholm, Sweden—

DOCTOR ÖSTEN UNDÉN: When I was asked to participate on Armistice Day in a broadcast program on the subject "The Family of Nations," I was at Geneva as Swedish delegate to the League of Nations. It was during those September days when the clouds of a new world war were hanging heavily over us. In no way whatever was the League of Nations entrusted with the task of dealing with the critical situation which was then prevailing. It was more obvious than ever that the League was quite powerless to make a contribution to the peaceful solution of the controversy.

Germany was no longer a member of the League, it is true. But there existed, and still exists, a treaty between Germany and Czechoslovakia, according to which all disputes without exception shall be settled by peaceful means. The treaty stipulates the different methods of procedure to be employed, arbitration for questions of a legal nature, mediation before a commission of conciliation—ultimately before the Council of the League of Nations—for all other kinds of disputes. I am myself one of the three neutral members of that commission of conciliation, and my mandate was renewed the last time in 1936, for three years. Furthermore, Germany and Czechoslovakia and also Poland and Hungary are signatories to the Pact of Paris.

Instead of negotiations, armed force was used as a threat and as an instrument of policy. The pledged word was disregarded. Finally the governments of four great Powers dictated the partition of Czechoslovakia. Not only the people of Czechoslovakia, but all adherents of order under law in international relations, must have been deeply shocked by this recklessness.

Peace was saved. The settlement at Munich undoubtedly brought about a world-wide feeling of relief on account of our having escaped another war. But that feeling of relief was very much mixed with feelings of bitterness and humiliation because the settlement had taken place under such disgusting forms and on such ruthless terms. It is, indeed, a piece of historical irony that the Germans, who for twenty years have complained —and with justification—of the methods which were employed against them after their defeat in the Great War, should now themselves employ similar methods against a weaker state. That peace which was concluded at Munich was not one of reconciliation. Therefore we dare not hope that it foreshadows the dawn of a new era.

In my country, and in many others that have been keen supporters of the League of Nations, the experiences of the past few years have shaken our faith in the practicability of the League's actual system of "Collective Security," such as is outlined in Article 16 of the Covenant. That system, when confronted with reality, has broken down. Our states, therefore, consider themselves justified in regaining their liberty of action so as to enable them to conduct a neutral policy in the event of a general war between the groups of great Powers. At least half of the League's members have made declarations in this sense.

This attitude does not, however, signify that our countries consider that the idea of a League of Nations is wrong, or that they believe the policy of neutrality and isolation to be the definite and real solution of the problem of safeguarding peace. Complete neutrality means that war is tolerated, that one is resigned to it as a fact. Such a policy within the Family of Nations means that if some members of the Family happen to engage in a life-and-death struggle, the other members turn their backs on the drama in the illusory hope of not being affected by it. Security can be obtained only through common efforts within an international organization.

Here in Europe we often turn our gaze toward the United States of America as being perhaps capable to aid us to get free from our pathological war complex. In his admirable address of June 3 of this year, Mr. Cordell Hull, the Secretary of State of the United States of America, has declared that he could wish for his country no more glorious course than to be a leader in devotion to the principles of international law, resting upon the foundation of co-operation, justice and morality. I, personally, believe that the great majority of the League's members would gladly accept practically any change in the structure and clauses of the League of Nations if we could thereby be assured of hearing the calm, passionless voice of the United States of America in our councils, repressing our internal quarrels. That great democracy which has succeeded in assimilating so many types of people from the various European countries would be able to infuse a living spirit in a recreated League of Nations.

I am thankful for the opportunity of directing these personal words to an American audience.

ANNOUNCER: We return you now to America—

DOCTOR BUTLER: By great good fortune we shall today hear the voice of that man who is leading the liberal thought of the world toward the establishment of those international economic policies which alone can restore prosperity to our several peoples and thereby strengthen the foundations on which international peace must always rest. Distinguished jurist and economist, trained at the University of Louvain in Belgium and at Princeton, one time Professor of Law at the University of Louvain, delegate to international economic conferences without number, Prime Minister and Minister for Foreign Affairs and Foreign Commerce in the years 1935 to 1937, Doctor Paul van Zeeland has established an honorable reputation which is fortunately world-wide and steadily increasing. I have the very great honor to present Doctor Paul van Zeeland, formerly Prime Minister of Belgium. We take you now to Tulsa, Oklahoma—

DOCTOR VAN ZEELAND: Today's twentieth anniversary of the great event, Armistice Day, should be enveloped with greater ceremony than ever before. It should be celebrated in an atmosphere of satisfaction and of hope. But I wonder whether this will be the case everywhere? Let us recall the dreams we were enjoying, the firm expectations we were envisaging twenty years ago —at the end of the war. If we should compare those high and legitimate hopes with the changed situation in which we find ourselves today, following twenty years of "post-war" trials, mishaps and missed opportunities, the realization of our deception indeed would be heavy to bear.

Most of us went into the war, and stood through it, with one shining ideal: We were fighting to deliver mankind from the horrors of war; we were ready to accept any sacrifice in order to help build another world of

peace, of mutual understanding, for our children. The
victory represented, in our eyes, mainly that possibility.
In spite of many errors, the Peace Treaty contained two
hints, two suggestions: first, a principle of organization
of mutual relations among nations, on a plane of equality
and reciprocity of rights and liabilities; second, an undertaking to disarm, or at least to limit armaments as far
as possible.

Today, the warriors of 1918 have grown old. When
they meet, crosses and medals go together with bald
heads, gray hair, and often sad eyes. The armament race
is speeding up again at a revived and tremendous pace.
The men of good will, even the more pacifist, have had
to realize that unilateral disarmament or non-armament
was leading to war still more inevitably than reciprocal
armaments. And we are yet under the strong impression that war in a new form, distinctly modern, *i.e.*, more
bloody, more blind, more atrocious than ever, has just
missed us by the thickness of a razor blade. After twenty
years, are we, or are we not, farther in the good direction than we were in 1914—than we were in 1918?

Yes, we are, in spite of all. Very distant, without
doubt, from the stage at which we should have been a
long while ago, but—still before us is an open road.
Nothing essential, so far, has been lost definitely; infinite
possibilities are yet ahead of us.

All the countries of the world, without exception, have
shown recently how deep-seated is the innate love for
peace in their hearts.

Recent political events have practically put an end to
the order established at Versailles. A new order has not
yet been created. Such is the task of tomorrow, at the

latest—of today, if it were possible. Peace will last, only if we hasten to organize its bases, both politically and economically. For that, there are no other methods than those so constantly advocated by the speakers at this tribune—mutual knowledge, reciprocal understanding, abolition of hatred, of despite and domination of spirit, and removal of artificial barriers to trade. These words may sound queer in the ranting clatter of arms. Yet they must keep their full meaning with their utmost importance, if we really want to avoid war.

Science is day after day rendering our world smaller, drawing together materially peoples and men throughout the world, providing ceaselessly new possibilities for an altogether general upward movement toward better material conditions of life. Each of us can help a bit in providing his share toward a spiritual uplift. Let us hope today, as strongly as ever, that peoples throughout the world will realize for all practical purposes how closely connected are their own profound interests, the progress of mankind as a whole, the material and moral ascension of millions of human beings and the ineradicable will for a lasting peace.

DOCTOR BUTLER: The next voice to which we are privileged to listen is that of a distinguished officer of the American Army, Commander of the Twenty-Seventh Division of the Expeditionary Force in France and Belgium, whose great service has been recognized and rewarded not alone by his own government but by that of Great Britain, of France, of Belgium and of Italy. I have the honor to present Major General John F. O'Ryan, speaking from New York.

GENERAL O'RYAN: My message is short. It is also definite. If you accept its conclusion, then you have the answer to the question "What can we do to suppress war?"

First let me remind you that war is not a calamity of
nature. It is a man-made calamity. And this man-made
calamity is infinitely more destructive to all that is best
in civilized life than are the worst visitations of nature;
worse, in other words, than fire, flood, earthquake, and
epidemic disease.

For generations, the remote consequences of war, even
more than its immediate evils, have been lowering the
capacity of millions of men to think logically, until today, many governments, meaning the few individuals
who actually constitute them, find it necessary, either
forcibly to regiment their subjects in masses and do their
thinking for them as if they were expensive domestic
animals, or to govern them by romance, by which is
meant through their instincts, appetites and emotions;
by folk-songs, largesse, nostrums and the distractions
created by induced hatreds and prejudices. Unhappily,
a high percentage of the masses in most countries is intellectually underprivileged. The point is that this class
is increasing in disproportion to the increase of population. While this is due in part to medical science, which
has progressively defeated the aim of nature to eliminate
the unfit, their existence is nevertheless substantially
traceable to the wars of past centuries, for war shelters
the mentally, morally and physically unfit by leaving
them at home, while it imposes its processes of whole-
sale homicide upon the physically and mentally fit young
men of the nations at war. Worse still, war destroys the
masses of its battle victims at an age when for the most

part they are unmarried and childless, and leaves the
procreation of the race to those at home, including the
morons, drunkards, mentally deficient and the diseased.
And nature ordains that in substantial measure the descendants of the unfit perpetuate the mental and physical
defects of their forebears. Thus, one of the remote consequences of war is to pass on to succeeding generations
an apparently increasing percentage of the unfit, to become the economic wards of the fit. War is indeed the
most relentless and insidious enemy of mankind. And
if you, my listeners, who have fit sons take no organized
action to substitute world law and order for war, you are
playing the criminal role of accessories before the fact
to the slaying of your own sons in the next war.

And now to the remedy. War *is* a complex problem,
but its complexities are not basic. They lie in the field
of human ambitions, traditions and fears. But all progress has been confronted by such obstacles. The institutions of slavery and dueling existed from time im-
memorial until recently, but the progress of civilization
suppressed them. So it will be with war. It is only a
question of time. Why wait? I have said that the obstacles to peace are in the field of human ambitions,
hatreds and fears. These cannot be eliminated by wish-
ful thinking. They can, however, be controlled, and
that is all that is necessary. Consider for a moment a
typical example. We know that millions of people living today in various European countries are so organized
that by the mere push of a button they can be caused to
abandon their families and jobs and, with little or
specious understanding of why they do so, march forth
to destroy one another by bullet, bomb, and gunfire. Is

it not of compelling interest to reflect upon the known
fact that these same hostile peoples, or those of them
who emigrate to this country, are caused by our laws to
live peacefully as neighbors even in our crowded cities?
*They become peaceful because compelled to do so by
law that can be and is enforced.* And in the course of a
few decades, they may be found as members of the same
Rotary or other club, and still later, not infrequently,
they witness the intermarriage of their respective sons
and daughters. *Abie's Irish Rose* is merely symbolic of
what has been going on for fifty years in this country
among the descendants of the warring peoples of Europe. The change results because these people are compelled by our neutral laws to keep the peace, and our
laws are backed by organized courts of justice *and* by a
police power adequate to meet any challenge. There
you have the key principle underlying world peace. The
truth is that these immigrants had no option about being
orderly and peaceful, and it was not long before they
recognized this, and their common sense prompted the
rest. And so it was with the original states of our Union.
Although they are sovereign powers with widely diver-
gent climate, natural resources and economic interests,
they were not permitted to make war one against another. The covenant we call the Federal Constitution
prohibits it, and the police power behind that covenant
is adequate to enforce the prohibition.

The same principles apply with added force when we
consider the maintenance of peace among the nations of
the world. If they want peace, they can have it by common agreement in the form of a basic code, covenant or
treaty which provides not only for an executive body, a

legislative body, and a world court, but also for an international police power adequate to enforce peace.

There is no other solution of the world problem. None. But world organization, even if effectuated by all other powers, cannot succeed without the complete membership of the United States. It was our absence from membership in the League of Nations, as well as the lack of a definite and adequate police power, which wrecked the League. If we are not ready to accept membership in a world organization for the maintenance of world peace, then we are not ready for world peace and we should quit our meaningless lip service to peace and our talk in relation to armaments and other evils that necessarily are collateral features of a world in training for war.

Ninety per cent of the people of the world want a world organized for peace in lieu of a world organized for war. Such, however, is the present state of world psychology that any suggestion by a European power for a conference to bring this about would be futile. Only the United States could request such a conference with any hope for success. Such a request from us will be premature until our people understand that the initiative for organized world peace rests with us and that our membership is essential. If we are not ready for this, then we must realistically accept the alternative. There is no middle course. The alternative demands real preparation for war, a substantial increase in armaments and universal military training. Anything else would be folly. In a war world, the best security is to be prepared for war. It was to such a world this admonition of Washington was applied.

Therefore, my friends, if you want world peace, you can have it by awakening the understanding and the conscience of the American people in relation to the foregoing principles and facts. Organize from coast to coast to do this. Do not bother the President. He understands the problem. Do not petition the Congress, which awaits only the voice of the people. Organize and express the universal demand of the families of America for world peace in terms of world organization and power to enforce it. The families of Europe will echo the demand.

DOCTOR BUTLER: May the many millions of men and women who in all parts of the civilized world have heard these eloquent and inspiring addresses on this Armistice Day be moved so to act as to translate their faith into public policy.

The history of civilization might be written in terms of man's progress from fear to faith. As he has ceased to fear his neighbors and as he has come to have trust in them, he has been able to build up institutions that have lasted. Just as the individual has substituted faith in his fellow man for fear of him, so nations may well divest themselves of fear in favor of faith in the other nations of the world.

The United States has done so much to educate world opinion in the past century and a half that we may well be ambitious for it to do still more. We have shown that to all appearances a federal form of government, extended over a wide area and embracing many competing and sometimes conflicting interests, is practicable, and that it can survive even the severe shock of civil war.

We have shown that under the guidance of a written constitution, judicially interpreted, there is room for national growth and expansion, for stupendous economic development, for absorption into the body politic of large numbers of foreign born, and for the preservation of civil liberty over a considerable period of time. Suppose now that during the next few decades it might be given to us to lead the way in demonstrating to the world that great sovereign nations, like federated states, may live and grow and do business together in harmony and unity, without strife or armed conflict, through the habit of submitting to judicial determination all questions of difference as they may arise, the judicial decree when made to be supported and enforced—after the fashion in which judicial decrees are everywhere supported and enforced—by intelligent public opinion and by an international and neutral police. Might we not then be justified in believing that the place of our beloved country in history was secure?

XI

NEW YEAR MESSAGE, 1939

A New Year message for the *New Way*,
the official organ of the
Industrial Peace Union of the British Empire,
November–December, 1938

NEW YEAR MESSAGE, 1939

The year 1938 has been one of grievous disappoint-
ment, but we must not weaken our faith or lose our
courage. For the time being, force has won victory over
law and public morals, and the constructive progress
which was making toward an organized family of nations has been checked. We must address ourselves without delay with the utmost earnestness toward repairing
the damage which has been done to those foundations
on which alone a prosperous and a peaceful world can
permanently rest. The League of Nations must be re-
constructed as an organized family of nations without
any regard to the Treaty of Versailles, and looking forward, not backward. There is no use in wasting argument to fix the blame for that which is past; we must
now face the future in a spirit of hopeful confidence.
First of all, the intelligent peoples of the world must
require their governments to keep the faith when their
word has been plighted. Formal engagements between
nations must be regarded as are contracts between individuals and not to be broken through force or threats
of force. The mind of the world must be turned toward
the promotion of agriculture, industry and commerce,
and toward that international exchange which, through
uniting various national interests, quickly produces the
international mind. This, as I defined it long ago, is
nothing other than that habit of thinking of foreign
relations and business, and that habit of dealing with

them, which regard the several nations of the civilized world as friendly and co-operating equals in aiding the progress of civilization, in developing commerce and industry, and in spreading enlightenment and culture throughout the world.

The international mind requires that faith and confidence be re-established, that differences between nations and their governments be settled through conference, negotiation or arbitration, and, when necessary, be appealed to the formal judicial process before the stately Permanent Court of International Justice set up at The Hague. The federal principle, as applied in the government of the United States and, in another form, in the government of the British Commonwealth of Nations, is now to be applied to the construction of an organized Society of Nations, with its capital at Geneva. The record of events plainly shows that the peoples of the world are in almost every land far in advance of the action and the policies of their governments. The peoples must compel their governments to do their will an undertake those policies, national and international which mean prosperity and peace. From an economic point of view, it is quite misleading to say that the world is suffering from over-production. What the world is suffering from is under-consumption. Surely there can be no over-production when men, women and children in any part of the world are starving or ill-clothed o most improperly housed. Better distribution must follow upon growing production. When this is done, consumption will increase rapidly. Let us hope that 1935 will tell a better and happier story.

XII

EDUCATION FOR PEACE

An address at the dinner for University Presidents,
University Club, New York,
January 20, 1939

EDUCATION FOR PEACE

Mr. President, This most distinguished company of guests and my fellow members of the University Club:

To stand in this presence for a few moments this evening is a genuine inspiration. To reflect upon what this company represents, and what it means in our American life, strengthens one's hope and confidence and relieves one's anxieties as he looks out over this troubled and difficult world.

For these guests, honorable and experienced captains in our nation's real army of defense, and this company coming as it does from institutions of learning all over this land, inspired by a common purpose, bound together by like traditions, background, experience and interest, reflects all that is best in our American life.

At no time in my life—and I am disposed to think at no time in three hundred or four hundred years—has the world witnessed such a widespread lack of confidence and feeling of uncertainty and depression in every relationship as that which exists at this moment. I have frequently used the illustration, and I may repeat it again in your presence, of the extraordinary significance of the famous cartoon which Sir John Tenniel contributed to *Punch* in the month of March, 1890. That cartoon represented Bismarck going over the side of the Ship of State and the young Kaiser standing on the bridge ready to take command of the ship when the old captain should have gone. It was called "Dropping the

Pilot." It has been reproduced a thousand times from that day to this, and the lesson which it teaches is highly significant for all of us. It is not for Germany alone, but for the world.

That lesson is that about the end of the nineteenth century a new era began, a new era in the world intellectual, a new era in the world economic, a new era in the world social, a new era in the world political. There then began to come to a climax the results of the stupendous additions to scientific knowledge which had been going on for nearly a century and which have now revolutionized the whole industrial and economic system of the civilized peoples. From that day to this we have been trying, so far in vain, effectively to readjust our life and our occupations to those new conditions. Then there came new aspirations in the field of politics, some of them national, some of them international. These began to take on various forms of vigorous expression in different parts of the world. Finally they came to their climax in the World War.

We shall never be able to understand what that war cost us. Of course we are familiar with the figures so frequently cited of what it cost in terms of money. We are familiar with what it cost in terms of human life. But what we have not yet begun to grasp is what it cost in terms of the intellectual life, of fundamental principles and of moral standards.

If we were to look at this world from a distance and without the inspiration which we of this country are so fortunate as to possess, we might well feel compelled to surrender to a hopeless pessimism. The cynic and the pessimist would have his way and we should be invited to sit and watch the world go to pieces. In the presence of this company, it may be frankly said that we know better than that.

We know what the answer is. We know where relief is to be found. It is to be found in the training and discipline of human intelligence, of free men and free women able, because of what they understand of what has been, to face with capacity and confidence that which is to be.

We forget, because the process of college education is so familiar to us, how new it is and how splendidly it has served mankind and particularly the American people during the years of its existence. I may say that in many ways the American college is the most important institution in our public life. It exists by the score, large and small, rich and struggling, east and west, north and south, but everywhere under the same inspiration, with the same purpose, the same ideals, and aiming at the same high public service.

The American college is peculiarly and particularly American. This company could not be assembled in any other country in the world, not even in Great Britain. On the continent of Europe it would be wholly unknown. Our college is the fruit of the independent development on this side of the Atlantic, of the idea and the example of the colleges of Oxford and of Cambridge as they existed in the seventeenth and eighteenth centuries. That college has developed, not as a residential unit of a large and many-sided corporation as at Oxford and Cambridge, but as a single independent self-governing institution set in its own environment, reaching its own constituency, pursuing its own methods and

aiming at its own ideals. It has steadily grown in power
and in influence. On the continent of Europe there is
nothing of any kind, sort or description to correspond
with the American college. The Gymnasium, the Gin-
násio, the Lycée and the Liceo are very different from
the college. They lead directly to the university with
its large *Lernfreiheit* and its devotion to scientific research for its own sake.

These four precious years of college life and work
which we have built up and developed, in part out of
the Gymnasium, in part out of the beginnings of the
university, are the years which we devote to a liberal
education. Their aim is not vocational training, not any
specific pursuit, but a liberal education, an education
worthy of a free man in a free state. That liberal education is the background of progress now and always and
as we produce from these institutions year by year hundreds and thousands of trained young men and women,
we shall be arming our country for the struggle which
is before it. For the colleges are the real armament
factories of a free democracy. There you have the instruments of contest and of victory for the use of the
trained and educated human beings.

And what is it for which we are arming? Every nation in the world, free and dictatorial, is arming. What
for? They are all for peace. They are all devoted to
peace. Under no circumstances could there be anything
for them but peace; and yet the whole resources of these
peoples are devoted to preparing for that in which they
say that they do not believe, which they will not have
and to which they will never consent. Are we mad?
Do we need to go into an asylum for the care of the

insane or is there some great gap between us? Is there
some bridge which we have not built? Is there some
path which we have not learned to follow?

Had we not better begin to ask that question and press
it home and to prepare these youths who come to us for
training and for discipline to answer that question themselves and to guide public opinion toward its constructive answer? We are accustomed, we Americans and the
English-speaking people generally, to take a great many
things for granted which the rest of the world does not
accept for a moment. If they accept these things at all
they accept them orally or verbally but not with any true
understanding or with any real conviction.

What is really at stake in the world underneath and
behind peace and prosperity? What is really at stake is
liberty. If you will go back to Aristotle, you will begin
to find how long that contest has been going on and how
real it is. But you say that nobody can be opposed to
liberty.

In a conversation, a rather exciting conversation,
which I had some years ago with the head of the government of Italy, I said something about liberty, that a great
many people thought liberty was dying. He said to
me with great emphasis, "Dying? Liberty is not dying.
It is dead!" We proceeded to argue that question with
earnestness and the widest possible difference of opinion
for some time.

When the head of the government of a country tells
you that liberty is dead and believes it, there is something of a challenge to the American people, their institutions and their education.

Those of us who have seen many passing years are

not going to live to see the conclusion of this struggle.
It is going to take a long time, but I hope that the
younger men, charged with the direction and oversight
of these great power-houses of learning and character-
building, may see the successful result of their efforts
and the establishment on a new and firm basis of those
fundamental principles of life and morals which must
rule, with gain-seeking in secondary place. The American
college, as the training place for the leaders of the next
generation, has a responsibility and a difficult problem
far in excess of any of those which the older men or their
predecessors have ever known.

We shall need all the experience of our Harvard and
William and Mary, Yale and Pennsylvania, Princeton
and Columbia, Rutgers and Dartmouth, which began
their history before the Declaration of Independence;
we shall need all the experience and power of the admirable institutions of younger years that have come to
join that older group, to give support to the American
ideals; to the American determination in terms of understanding what political principles mean, how they have
been developed through the ages, and what relation they
bear to the problems of today with a view to the reconstruction of a peaceful, a prosperous and a happy plan of
life and work for the whole world.

XIII

WHERE IS TO BE THE NEXT CAPITAL OF THE WESTERN WORLD?

An address delivered at the annual meeting
of The Pilgrims of the United States, Bankers Club,
New York, January 25, 1939

WHERE IS TO BE THE NEXT CAPITAL OF
THE WESTERN WORLD?

My Fellow Pilgrims: This troubled and distracted world upon which we look must soon give answer to the most important question which can be put to it. The answer to that question may well control the development of western civilization for five hundred years.

This world is a world at war. In its every part, it is at war, either military or economic. In addition, it is everywhere making colossal preparation for war at appalling cost to the earnings and the savings of the people, and with disastrous results to the social, the economic and the political order of the several nations.

The question which must be answered is this: Where is to be the next capital of the western world? By capital I do not mean the center of purely political organization; I mean the center from which shall go out that stream of influence, of ideals, of principles and of policies which will guide and shape civilization for the period into which we are passing through this revolution.

The world, this western world, has had three capitals. The first was ancient Athens. From that amazing city on the Acropolis and about it there went out for four hundred years the stream of influence in the intellectual life, in philosophy, in literature, in science, in the fine arts, in ideals, which stirred and shaped the world forever. Athens passed as a capital itself, but the influences which it set in motion are at work among us all today.

Athens was followed by Rome. That truly colossal center of power and of influence ruled the western world for five hundred years. It ruled it in terms of law, in terms of administration, in terms of public service. It solved the problem of governing minorities; it solved the problem of building roads and bridges and tunnels, and bringing distant parts of the world in touch with one another. It solved the problem of a uniform system of government with plenty of elasticity for local and regional conditions, and it solved the problem of a regard and reverence for law.

Then Rome passed, and for a thousand years the western world was without an effective intellectual capital. Constantinople tried to establish itself, but in vain. Paris undertook the same task but was not able to accomplish it for any great length of time. Charlemagne thought he could have a capital at what is now Aix-la-Chapelle, but that proved impossible.

It was a thousand years before the third capital appeared in the city of London. Following the defeat of the Spanish Armada and the great administration of Queen Elizabeth and the statesmen whom that era developed, London became the center of the controlling force in the intellectual guidance of the modern world.

England took to the sea. She bound the distant parts of the world together. Long before there was any Suez Canal, her ships had gone around the Cape of Good Hope, to Eastern Africa, to India, China and Japan, and then to Australia and New Zealand, to say nothing of the Americas. She developed not only the system of civil liberty predicted by Magna Carta and carried forward by the Petition of Right and the Bill of Rights, but she did all that in the field of commerce and industry and finance—something unknown to the Greeks, unknown to the Romans—and the world became a vast industrial-commercial establishment with the moving force in London itself.

That era has plainly come to an end. It has come to an end largely as the effect of the industrial revolution which began over a hundred years ago, and to which we have not yet been able to adapt our social, our economic and our financial systems.

The historian who will write the story of this generation is almost certain to say that we are all mad, that we have shown complete incapacity to come face to face with the great economic and social problems of our time, and that because of that incapacity, because of feebleness of purpose and of will, this civilized world is wobbling and is in a position where it can be dealt with by dictators as our grandfathers would never have believed to be possible.

Where is the next capital going to be? From what part of the world is the next great stream of influence to go out to inspire, to guide and to control a constructive and progressive civilization? There is every sign that that capital may cross the Atlantic. That capital may find itself in another generation or two on the shores of this new land, so to speak, because that land has it in its power, with intelligence and moral courage, to make itself the outstanding exemplar of those policies of liberty, of progress and of human service which alone can save and develop our civilization.

And if that center of intellectual inspiration shall cross the Atlantic, to what point will it come? The United

States of America is one of the three great nations which created an artificial seat of government. India did this in putting New Delhi between Calcutta and Bombay. Australia did the same in putting Canberra between Sydney and Melbourne, and we did the same in putting the District of Columbia between Philadelphia and Richmond. That epoch-marking conversation between Thomas Jefferson and Alexander Hamilton on the street of Philadelphia, walking backward and forward before the residence of President Washington, determined that our seat of government should not be at any one of the centers of population, not even at Philadelphia, which was then chief among them all.

It may be that this new capital of thought and of inspiration and guidance may find itself on the Island of Manhattan. Why? Because, while not the seat of government, there is concentrated here and has been for one hundred and sixty years the nation's greatest power of constructive and guiding thought and of social and economic activity and inspiration.

If this capital should cross the Atlantic, if it should come to the Island of Manhattan, what an obligation and what an opportunity will rest upon us, our children and our grandchildren!

What is the guidance we shall be called upon to give? My Fellow Pilgrims, that guidance is all written out for us in the four hundred and sixty-one immortal words which constitute the Bill of Rights of the Federal Constitution. We need not add to them, we need not amend them. They are the Magna Carta of the twentieth century. What Magna Carta did seven hundred years ago, and the high place which it has occupied in the history of liberty, can now be done and repeated by our Bill of Rights for the next great period if we, the American people, guided and inspired by our leaders of thought and action in this great city and in our other great communities, can have the courage, the intelligence and the zeal for public service to seize upon that Bill of Rights, to apply it to ourselves at every moment, no matter what temptation there may be to violate it, and to press it upon the civilized world. Then the great struggle for the control of the human race will pass into the terms of a struggle between the Bill of Rights and those who do not believe in the fundamental principles of political, social and economic liberty.

But we are not going to make any progress by sitting still. We are not going to make any progress by the mere use of words. It is incumbent upon us to demonstrate, day by day, month by month and year by year, what the Bill of Rights means when translated into terms of practical and everyday life, and to preach that, to teach that, to demonstrate that to those peoples who for one motive or another, because of one vast emotion or another, have been for the time being put under the heel of the cruel and relentless despot.

The choice, my Fellow Pilgrims, is between the Bill of Rights and despotism. The leadership must come from the United States of America!

XIV

WORLD CONDITIONS WE ARE FACING

An address delivered before the Men's Bible Class of the
Riverside Church, Hotel Commodore, New York,
February 14, 1939

WORLD CONDITIONS WE ARE FACING

Doctor Fosdick and Gentlemen: To stand for a few moments this evening in the presence of this noteworthy assemblage, so obviously representative of what is best in the citizenship of our great capital city, is truly an inspiration. For the honor of your invitation and for the opportunity which it offers, I extend to you an expression of my most grateful appreciation.

It has been suggested that I should say something as to the world conditions in which we are living and which we are facing. Every adjective which can be thought of has been applied to these conditions by somebody during the past three or four years.

One difficulty with our problems is that we are lacking in the right kind of leadership to enable us to proceed to their solution, the reason for which is that, under the pressure of modern conditions and the modern social order—the telegraph, the telephone, the radio, and the newspaper—we are tempted to live only in the happenings of the moment. We are concerned with the news, with what has just taken place; and we find little opportunity—and, I am sorry to say, little inclination—to go behind the news and ask what are its causes and what explanation may be given of it.

As a matter of fact, these extraordinarily difficult and complicated problems which face the world of today are not, in any correct sense of the word, new. They are new in their form, for obvious reasons, but fundamentally they are an expression and a revelation of an age-long conflict in human nature and human society which forms the background of the history of western civilization.

Our troubles began at the Tower of Babel. When languages were multiplied and men were dispersed, the problem of organizing the world had its beginning—organizing it on a plane of high ideals, of knowledge, of faith, of human service—and that movement has been going on from the day of the Tower of Babel until this.

We fail sometimes to look at the great moving forces in history which, should we look at them, illuminate in very large measure the practical and definite problems which face us day by day. When western civilization began its course, the ruling idea was that the whole of the civilized world should be brought under one rule, and that the rule of a great military captain. This was in the mind of Alexander the Great, when he left Greece to cross Persia on his way to India. This was in the mind of Julius Cæsar when he left Italy to conquer Gaul, and found himself in possession of part of what is now Great Britain.

That movement to unify the world, to bring it under one government, with one set of rules or laws and one great central administration, broke down with the fall of Rome. There followed the next step, which was nation-building. Since all these peoples could not be brought together under one government, the notion took form and shape that they might be grouped and organized in nations.

What is a nation? A nation, as I have often said, is defined as an ethnic unity which inhabits a geographic unity. In terms of that very technical and admirable definition, there are few, if any, nations, for the reason that the movement of mankind over the earth has practically prevented the long continuance of anything like ethnic unity. The races have become intermixed through marriage not only over generations but through centuries.

So we have to content ourselves with the conception of ethnic unity which would mean a large ethnic majority inhabiting a geographic unity or trying to control one; and if you take the history of Europe and the United States and South America from the fall of Rome to to-day, you can write it in terms of that movement.

A geographic unity is easily defined and observed. Italy is a geographic unity, protected on the north by the Alps, on the east by the Adriatic, on the south and west by the Mediterranean. The Spanish peninsula—Spain and Portugal—is a geographic unity, protected on the north by the Pyrenees, surrounded by the Mediterranean, the Strait of Gibraltar, and the Atlantic. The British Isles are a geographic unity. Scandinavia is a geographic unity. And, if there had been in Central Europe a high row of mountains or a very wide sea, we should have avoided nine out of ten of the wars which have arisen and been carried on in that part of the world during the last thousand years.

The desire of a nation to unify itself, to get rid of elements that were not liked, that had some different point of view, that had a different background, or its desire to get possession of a given point of adjacent territory because it completed a geographic unity—that is all part of the process of nation-building. We are watching it now in the most extreme form which it has ever taken—that is, in the case of the Third Reich.

But what is happening there is not new. Recall, if you will, the history of the Protestant movement in France. You have only to go back something less than four hundred years to the Massacre of St. Bartholomew, one of the most terrible and destructive assaults by men upon men that history records. After that, Henry IV wrote the Edict of Nantes, and he protected religious liberty and religious freedom for a hundred years. Then, when Louis XIV nullified that Edict of Nantes, the Huguenots had to leave France. Most of them came to the United States. Sailing from the Port of Rochelle, in France, they settled New Rochelle, in Westchester County; they came into Pennsylvania; they came to Charleston, South Carolina—as refugees, precisely as Jews and Catholics and other persecuted groups are coming today out of that Third Reich.

In other words, these fundamental causes and fundamental movements have to be reckoned with, not as something transitory, but as new revelations, new manifestations, of something that is deep down in the history of the human race, and which has its roots in human nature, and which can be conquered and governed only by the highest type of intelligence and the highest type of faith.

We see this process going on, and we see the head of a government, or a government, waiting for opportunity to go just a little farther to increase the boundaries of what that government believes to be a geographic unity, or in a direction which will take in an element of population which that government believes to be part of its ethnic unity. There you have the story of what has been going on for over a thousand years, and which today, instead of being new, is the same old contest, the same old conflict, under circumstances so extraordinary that the results and effects are far more appalling than they ever have been earlier in the history of the human race.

What is all this about? Why do these peoples wish to unify themselves in a geographic unity in the neighborhood of their home? The answer is, first, that they may have the sources of livelihood, the necessities of existence. The second is that they may find what they conceive to be the geographic essentials of protection against attack from without.

Look at our own history in the United States. Our thirteen colonies here on the fringe of the Atlantic seemed a very important group of people, and, when organized, to be a very considerable nation. But the Northwest Territory, Florida, the country that belonged to Mexico, Texas, and up in the Northwest, the country that belonged to England—with one piece after another we proceeded to build our geographic unity into its present form. We took the Atlantic, the Gulf of Mexico, the Rio Grande, the Pacific, as our boundaries and then that wonderful line which is the most significant boundary line in the world, because, without a fort and without a camp, it has been for a century and a quarter a sign of how civilized people can live side by side, maintaining their ethnic unity, without resort to war or the rule of force.

That nation-building process will go on, I assume, until the time shall come—and I wish, indeed, it might come soon; twenty years ago we thought it had arrived —when these nations, instead of attempting to prey upon one another, to take advantage of one another, either in a military or in an economic sense, shall find it possible to bind themselves together in a world federation that will do for them all that our national federation did for us one hundred and fifty years ago.

There is no other solution of the world problem in terms of prosperity and peace, and the longer it is postponed, the more difficult will its achievement be, the greater will be the loss in human life, and the greater the disturbance and distress to our civilization.

One looks for some clew to what lies behind the problems of these various nations, our own included. We state our problems in one way, Great Britain states its problems in another, France states its problems in another, Germany in another, Italy in another, Japan in another, China in another—but, fundamentally, those problems all arise at a point which it is not difficult to describe.

A nation, I repeat, in its perfect form, is an ethnic unity inhabiting a geographic unity, but that nation is unorganized. It is just a people, moving about. The moment that nation becomes organized, it is a state. A state is the fundamental social and political organization of a nation. It may be arrived at—and generally is arrived at—unconsciously, without any formal steps. Long before men knew how to pass resolutions or to elect representative bodies, they brought into existence a crude form of social organization, and that was the state.

But, as civilization progressed, that state had to find some machinery for carrying on its business, some machinery for making life possible to its population, some machinery for playing its part in the world—and it had to set up a government. So it is, first the nation; then the state; and, finally, the government.

The government has been, time and time again, set up by a process of development, and without any formal act, without the meeting of any convention, without any exchange of letters, without any documentary evidence of any kind whatsoever. It has just come into existence, to meet the necessities of the case. Sometimes it has come into existence with an unwritten constitution, as in Great Britain. Sometimes—and, latterly, quite commonly—it has come into existence through a written constitution, as in the case of the United States, of France, and of almost all of the European nations after the Great War.

That government is not the state. The government plus the field of liberty is the state, and, in our constitution, we have taken pains to define very specifically the field of government, and to name definitely the things it could do. We have also put down, in black and white, what it cannot do and what we keep for ourselves.

Government plus liberty is the state. The government is not the state. To have a state, you must add to government, liberty; and, in America and Great Britain, we have always reserved, since Magna Carta, by far the larger field to liberty, leaving government a restricted and very definitely prescribed and defined field.

As time has gone on, these modern peoples have found themselves face to face with an entirely new set of external conditions which have modified the possible ways of operating these very fundamental principles. Down past the time of the institution of the government of the United States, conditions—economic and social and

political—were relatively simple; but just about that
time began those discoveries in science, in industry, and
in commerce, which brought about the industrial revolution. The industrial revolution was a means of providing
man with what he wanted for far less human labor than
had ever been the case before. The machine, operating
on a large scale, displaced any quantity of human effort.

The first important conflict betwen human labor and
the machine came in Lyons, France, the seat of the silk-
weaving industry. When the Jacquard loom was invented, one hundred and forty years ago, the streets of
Lyons were filled with shouting mobs who destroyed
every Jacquard loom that they could find. That was the
first, and violent, reaction on the part of the displaced
human labor against the new machine and the new mul-
tiform and manifold method of production.

A large part of our agricultural problem today is due
to the fact that where, not so long ago, in our Middle
Western and Northwestern country, it was possible to
find occupation for thousands, and hundreds of thousands, of farm owners and farm laborers, today the improved and remarkably efficient agricultural machinery
has displaced them by the thousands and the tens of
thousands.

That displacement of human industry by the machine
and by the machine process and by production on a huge
scale is the effect of an industrial revolution which is
now just about a hundred or one hundred and twenty
years old. A large part of the world's problem today
is how to adjust ourselves to that industrial revolution,
and it is because none of us has learned how to do it that
we have our economic problem.

One nation tries it in one way, another nation tries it in another, but, as yet, no people has found a solution of what is necessary, on the part of government and the state, to adjust the populations of this era to the results of the industrial revolution. This has led to one of the most extraordinarily reactionary movements which history records. It has led to an attempt at national economic isolation—buy nothing that is not made in your own country or in your own town or on your own block. Have nothing to do with any other nation, because, if you let them have anything, you will have to buy something back; if you buy back, you displace some product of your own.

That highly superficial argument has gone around the world, and today the world is at war from one end to the other. There are military wars, here and there— but the economic war is universal. Every nation is engaged in it.

If we were to be successful in waging an economic war on behalf of the United States, what would become of our twenty-five million or twenty-six million automobiles, not one of which could have been built and equipped if the elements had all to be produced within our national borders? What would become of our life, and the life of other peoples?

What has happened is that the dictators, who have come into existence as a result of the failure of their populations to deal with this problem, are attempting to use the extraordinary power which, for the time being, is in their hands, to force an addition to economic isolation which, without giving it up, will remedy some of its shortcomings. The very ingenious methods by which the German economists have tried to keep Germany isolated and economically aloof, and at the same time to find a way to sell abroad, are breaking down because of their artificiality.

When you look at this problem from the fundamental point of view—not from the happenings, however exciting or interesting, day by day—you see these great underlying causes are at work. If we are going to solve them in terms of liberty, if we are going to solve them in terms of the preservation of what we call free institutions, we must begin to busy ourselves much more actively than we have shown any signs of doing for fifty years.

Ever since the Civil War period closed, the American people have settled down to an attitude of contentment. "Our form of government is better than any other, we are wiser than any other; our country is rich; everything will be all right, don't worry." That system will not work. The time has come—and its evidences should be pretty convincing—when we must devote ourselves to trying to solve that problem in terms of liberty.

Of course, if a nation becomes discouraged, if a nation feels that it is being discriminated against and is powerless, if it feels that it has not, and cannot have, within its existing limits, the requirements for a fortunate and a happy and prosperous life, it almost invites the dictator. And a nation—even a wise and experienced and cultivated nation—will put up with a dictator just so long as he gives signs of solving this problem. But—mark my words—when it becomes clear that his dictatorial methods are not going to solve the problem, those peoples are going to turn of their own accord, and without force being applied by anybody, to another and a more constructive method of solution.

Go back over the history of the United States. Go back to those extraordinary debates in the Federal Constitutional Convention of 1787, which, fortunately, James Madison preserved for us with substantial completeness. Go back to the great arguments before the people by our leading statesmen of any party down to our Civil War. Watch them trying to avert that war. Watch them trying to find ways and means to solve the problems of human slavery through an unbroken nation.

Do you realize that that problem would have been solved without any trouble if it had not been for the invention of the cotton gin, which was one of the earliest steps in the industrial revolution? But when that came into existence, late in the eighteenth century, and the cheapest kind of labor—preferably slave labor—would be helpful in producing cotton at a cheap price, the whole picture changed.

Thomas Jefferson opposed slavery. One after another of the great Southern leaders of one hundred and fifty years ago opposed slavery. Slavery was really brought into existence, and fastened on us for sixty years, by the industrial revolution. And, when our great leaders of both parties and of every shade of opinion found it was impossible to settle the question without conflict, the conflict came.

It tore this country to pieces for four years. None of us can remember, personally, the details of that conflict; but many of us are old enough to remember its repercussions and its echoes in our younger years. Not only did the war itself last four years, but the effects of it upon public opinion and public life lasted a full genera- tion, and only recently has it passed away, and the coun- try became as united psychologically and economically as it is, on the surface, politically.

You are in this world as citizens of the greatest, the most powerful, nation on earth, and the one with the oldest and best-tested form of government. Do you realize that no government on earth is as old as ours? Our government is celebrating its one hundred and fiftieth anniversary. The government of Great Britain was made over by the Reform Bill of 1832, by the Parliamentary Representation Act of 1867, by the Par- liament Act of 1911, and by the British Commonwealth of Nations Act in 1931. The present government of the British Commonwealth of Nations is eight years old. The government of France has existed only since 1871. The government of Germany is new every morn- ing. The governments of most of the small countries were made over, either after the Napoleonic War or after the Great War of 1914–18.

Here we are, Americans, with this inheritance, with this body of conviction, with this history, participating to the full in these great underlying forces to which I have so briefly referred, representing their effect, their influence upon human institutions, upon human thought, and upon human conduct. Here we are, in a position in which the future of the world lies in our hands.

When people tell us to mind our own business, my answer is that our business is the business of all our fellow men, and that we do not stand by and permit slaughter, murder, arson, because the person offended does not happen to be our brother or our sister. We are in a position where the principles upon which our country is founded are proving their soundness, day by day. We have not always been wise ourselves, by any means, in the action that has been taken with the permission—quiet or otherwise—of our citizenship, but we have avoided changing or infringing upon those fundamental principles.

There are only four hundred and sixty-one words in the Bill of Rights, and they are the four hundred and sixty-one most important words in the world today. If we could get those four hundred and sixty-one words accepted by the other great peoples that are now struggling under dictatorships, we should be on our way toward a very different world within the memory and experience of very many persons within the sound of my voice.

What we have to contradict—not by argument or by words, which is futile, but by acts—is the statement which Mussolini made to me in conversation when we were arguing this matter. I had said something about liberty, that a great many people thought liberty was dying.

"Dying?" said Mussolini. "Liberty is not dying. It is dead."

That is the position which we have to confute, and we have to prove it by the way in which we conduct our government, by the way in which we conduct our own lives, and by the ideals toward which we guide, through education, the lives of those who are going to be the men and women of the generation that lies ahead of us.

It is a world problem. It is a thousand years old. The forces are easy to recognize, if you look deep enough for them, and we, one of their chief products, are in the fortunate position, by the happenings of the past one hundred years, of being able to take responsibility, through guidance, inspiration, and example, in the building of a really new world.

XV

THE FOUR FREEDOMS

An article written for *The New York Times*,
World's Fair Edition, March 5, 1939

THE FOUR FREEDOMS

There are many significant signs that the four hundred and sixty-one words which record the Bill of Rights in the Constitution of the United States have become the most important of any words having to do with men's social, economic and political organization and institutions. Just as Magna Carta began in 1215 an era many centuries long marked by the steady, if slow, development away from absolute monarchy and a feudal system toward what has been recognized for some three hundred years as modern democracy, so this epoch-marking Bill of Rights may well have like service to perform.

The Four Freedoms which the Bill of Rights assures and defends are those of religion, of speech, of the press and of assembly. These four forms of freedom are in effect but four different aspects of one and the same form of freedom. They are those expressions of freedom which make it more than a mere word and raise it to the height of an institution. They name and define the fundamental rights which free men reserve to themselves as individuals when they set up an organized form of government and, either formally or by implication, grant to that government definite and prescribed powers. It must never be forgotten that individuals precede the state, which is the name for their organized form of social, economic and political life. Moreover, the state precedes government, which the individual citizens, acting as members of a state, set up to do certain definite and limited things.

The most clearly defined limitation upon the powers

and authority of the government of a free people is that set in the language of the Bill of Rights. To attempt to overturn the Bill of Rights, or to undermine it, is revolution. There is no possible public interest or public advantage to be gained by its damage or its overturn. The notion that every act by government is and must be in the public interest is grotesque. Every action by government, whether important or unimportant, is to be tested by public opinion, freely expressing itself under the Bill of Rights.

Today there are millions upon millions of human beings living under governments which not only do not accept the Four Freedoms, but frankly and openly deny them all. This is the result of a lust for power, and for power at any cost. This lust may take the form of economic regimentation or social control or political despotism, and wherever it exhibits itself the Four Freedoms are under attack.

There are those who clamor loudly for freedom of speech and freedom of assembly whose only concern is to use that freedom to undermine the foundations upon which it rests. Their aim is one or another of the forms of social, economic and political despotism.

It is imperative that at this vitally important turning point in the history of western civilization men and women everywhere shall study the history of the Bill of Rights and reflect upon its commanding significance. They must understand that it is constantly under attack, either openly or by indirection. The Bill of Rights needs the fullest protection by the free peoples of today in order that they may remain free peoples, and that the cause of freedom may not perish on the earth.

XVI

THE ENGLISH-SPEAKING PEOPLES SHOULD LEAD IN THE ESTABLISHMENT OF A WORLD SOCIETY OF NATIONS

Statement for the Anglo-American Supplement of
The Daily Telegraph, London, May 8, 1939

THE ENGLISH–SPEAKING PEOPLES SHOULD LEAD IN THE ESTABLISHMENT OF A WORLD SOCIETY OF NATIONS

From Anglo-Saxon days in England down to the building of the Federal Government of the United States of America, English history and English literature were one and the same on both sides of the Atlantic.

Following the independence of the American colonies, American history and American literature began their own development, separate and apart from the history and the literature of the peoples of Great Britain.

Unfortunately, from that time to this, while the American people have been taught English literature and no inconsiderable amount of English history, the English people have been taught practically nothing of American history and but very little of American literature.

Long experience has taught me that while the name of Washington is well known in England, and while the name of Lincoln is less well known, there is practically no knowledge of what principles and ideals these two names represent, and no knowledge of the political and social development of the American people and their contribution to world civilization.

One of the greatest needs of the present time is that the board schools in Great Britain, which are what we call public schools in the United States, shall give defi-

nite and well-ordered instruction to their pupils in the
political and social history, as well as in the literature,
of the people of the United States of America.

It is futile to ask for co-operation between two peoples, separated by more than three thousand miles of
ocean, who have merely nominal knowledge of each
other's history.

At the moment, the advantage lies with the people of
the United States. Their chief newspapers report more
fully day by day the important happenings in the public life of Great Britain than do the British newspapers
themselves. All important libraries in the United States
are thoroughly well provided with English books.

The one and only complete edition of the works of
John Milton, certainly the second name in the history
of English literature, is that which has just been published in the United States, following thirty years of devoted and laborious editorial work carried on in several
countries. Plans are under way for a similar edition of
the complete works of Edmund Burke, for which scholars have been waiting these many years.

It so happens that the story of the building of the
Federal Government of the United States is of the utmost importance at present. As I have frequently
pointed out, it was practically a laboratory experiment
in the great undertaking which now confronts the whole
world, namely, that of establishing a permanent and
orderly organized society of nations, on a new adaptation and application of the federal principle.

This principle has already been illustrated in admirable fashion by the Federal Government of the United
States of America and by the form of government set

up in 1931 by the Statute of Westminster for the British Commonwealth of Nations. It was also illustrated by the organization of the German Empire, guided by Bismarck, following the Franco-Prussian War of 1870. Each one of these three undertakings has a lesson to teach to the world of today, if only there be constructive statesmanship and leadership available to do the job.

There is no point in saying that such an ideal is unattainable. Were that true, civilization would now be going on the rocks and the dark ages would be illuminated in comparison with what must follow.

For four hundred years the conviction has prevailed among English-speaking peoples, and it has been justified by their own experience, that the fundamental principles of democracy were establishing themselves, certainly in the western world, and would be found adequate to meet the practical needs of modern civilized peoples.

From the beginning of the seventeenth century until well into the twentieth, the progress of these democratic principles and ideals was steady and successful. When the Great War broke in 1914, it quickly became obvious that behind and underneath all other differences and invitations to that massive struggle there lay a desperate conflict between these principles of democracy and their opponents. These opponents, which generations earlier had been under the leadership of absolute monarchs, now came under the leadership, first of aggressive and well-organized minorities, and then under that of dominating and relentless despots.

Today it is clear that everything for which the democratic nations fought in the Great War, and for which they made such appalling sacrifices of life and savings, has been lost. Indeed, the war itself has not come to an end, although it has for the time being changed its form and been shifted from the field of military operations to those of political rivalry and economic control.

What are the democracies going to do about it? Have they the moral courage, the intelligence and the leadership to carry on for another two or three hundred years the progress which was making, or will they tamely submit to being conquered, not by military war, but by threats and by the terror which threats inspire, as well as by economic penetration, and so give up the leadership of western civilization, letting their institutions go the way of the feudal system?

The most difficult task in the world is to make human beings think. This is something which they simply will not do, especially if they happen to belong to one of the English-speaking peoples. A Frenchman can be led to think, and before the German people lost, however temporarily, all their great characteristics, they could be led to think.

The English-speaking peoples, however, seem to regard thinking as something rather remote and unpractical. They consider it clever to deal with events as these come to their notice, without any understanding whatsoever of what the events mean, of how they have come to pass, or of what their consequences must certainly be.

Nothing is plainer than that at the moment the principles of democracy have had a world-wide check, and that with that fact and largely because of it morals and good faith have disappeared from the conduct of international relations. Solemn treaty obligations, long supposed to represent contracts between governments, are now tossed out of the window by one of the contracting parties with a nonchalance which is astounding.

If the democratic peoples are to protect themselves they must quickly find a way to do two things—they must recognize their community of interest and of ideals and they must proceed to organize a world-wide society of nations, using the existing League of Nations as a basis and point of departure.

If they will do this in a spirit of constructive liberalism they will find it possible to set up a federated family of nations to which the dictatorships, even if they do not collapse in the not distant future, will wish to belong, if only for economic reasons.

If the gain-seeking instinct cannot be controlled and guided by principles of morals and public service, then the democracies are without any hope, and no one can be wise enough to foretell what sort of a world is coming to supplant the one in which we live.

XVII

PEACE AND DEMOCRACY

An address delivered to the Graduating Class of
Columbia College on Class Day
June 5, 1939

PEACE AND DEMOCRACY

Following four years of carefully guided study and
ise personal counsel, you, members of the class to be
raduated tomorrow, are invited to enter the most
oubled and the most storm-tossed world which history
cords. Each one is to seek to find his place in that
orld, to take part in its activities and to give the whole
rce of his personality and his trained ability to its im-
rovement and to the solution of its truly colossal prob-
ms.

You have already heard much and you will continue
 hear much of Peace and Democracy. Peace and
emocracy are today the two most used words in the
nglish language. Rarely is either of them used ac-
urately. Peace does not mean the mere refraining from
ie use of military force of any kind as an alternative
 reasonable argument and to persuasion. A discrimi-
ating tariff is a form of war. A lock-out is a form of
ar. A strike is a form of war. Any other substitution
f force for argument and persuasion is war. It does not
ke long for any of these forms of economic, social or
olitical war to tempt recourse to military war. When
ne uses the word Peace, therefore, he must be sure that
e understands what that word really means.

Democracy, too, is recklessly used with little compre-
ension of its real meaning. Democracy does not mean
ie rule of the mob. Democracy does not mean that any
ajority, local or national, may do whatever it pleases

because of the fact that it is a majority. Democracy
government by the people, in the interest of all t
people, with guarantee of civil and religious liberty
every citizen. Without that guarantee, Democracy l
comes what Aristotle so long ago called Ochlocracy,
mob rule.

Given, then, a correct understanding of what the
two great words mean, it is evident that true Peace c
only be had if under a true Democracy public opini
guides government action on a plane that is reasonab
kindly, generous and constructive, and that refuses
make appeal to force.

The one legitimate, and indeed necessary, use
force by a true Democracy is when it represses and pu
ishes the criminal in its own ranks. This we call t
exercise of the police power and it has no resemblance
war and is no temptation to war.

Precisely the same is true in the field of internatior
relations. Where in those relations force is used,
should be only the collective force of an organized so
ety of nations serving as police power to repress
when necessary, to punish the law-breaker in the ran
of that organized society of nations.

There will be no real progress toward world pea
and toward that world prosperity which can only r
upon world peace, until these fundamental facts are u
derstood and accepted as guiding rules of condu
whether individual or national. When that time com
the world may have both Peace and Democracy.

For one hundred and eighty-five years the sons
this college have worked for Peace and for Democra
as leaders in every effort to advance and to achie

either of them. The great names whose monuments are all around about us—Hamilton and Jay and Livingston and Morris and Clinton and Hewitt—have all been written high on the roll of American patriots and American leaders, of both political thought and political action.

May each one of you, inspired by these names and by the public service with which they are associated, go forward to a life not only of useful and high-minded endeavor, but of achievement for the welfare of your fellow men.

XVIII

THE EVERLASTING CONFLICT

An address delivered at the 185th Commencement
of Columbia University
June 6, 1939

THE EVERLASTING CONFLICT

There is only one really fundamental problem which faces humankind. That problem underlies and conditions all other problems—ancient, medieval or modern —whether they have to do with the intellectual, the social, the economic or the political life of man. That problem exists because of the conflict between the spirit of man and the animal from which he has sprung and from which he is trying to free himself.

The life of the animal is shaped and controlled by the gain-seeking instinct in some one of its many forms of manifestation. That which is sought may be safety or nutriment or comfort or accumulation. This gain-seeking instinct not only naturally, but necessarily, accompanies the human being as he develops out of the animal and starts on what it is always hoped will be his higher and nobler career. For that career, the power of the gain-seeking instinct must always and everywhere be subordinate to the zeal for accomplishment in ultimate terms of human achievement and human service. If safety be sought, it must not be solely for purely personal or selfish reasons. If nutriment be sought, it must be in order that the strength gained shall find use in terms of helpfulness to fellow men. If comfort be sought, it must be for that satisfaction and leisure which prepare the way for larger and finer service to others. If accumulation be sought, it must be in order that wealth shall be distributed with sound judgment and fine instinct to aid in the accomplishment of noble human ends.

The unending human problem is one and the same; it is the struggle between the gain-seeking instinct and the desire for human service and accomplishment. There are no modern social problems save in the sense that the conditions under which this everlasting conflict is carried on are those of contemporary life. But in all essentials the conflict is always the same, one which has lasted through the ages and which gives every sign of lasting through the ages to come.

For any interpretation of human history there are two necessary assumptions. One is that there is such a thing as a moral order, and the other is that progress is possible. Without these two assumptions, human civilization could not exist. There would be nothing in the world but animal life and its various manifestations and changes.

That there is a moral order means that moral principle and moral ideals should take precedence of all else, and that there is progress means that man has had a certain measure of success in putting moral principle and moral ideals ahead of selfishness and gain-seeking as motives to conduct.

The philosophy of history contains many sad chapters, and some of these are very long. It records, time and again, that after a period of real progress, human civilization has stood still or even slipped backward because of the failure of mankind to uphold and to protect moral principle and moral ideals. It needs no profound philosopher to grasp the fact that the world in this day and generation is in one of these periods of reaction, perhaps the greatest. Selfishness and gain-seeking are assuredly controlling the policies of great nations called civilized, and their contempt for moral principle is as complete and as outspoken as if moral principle did not exist. Force and threats of force, made solely and always in support of gain-seeking and selfish advantage, are the ruling principle of public policy on the part of governments which are so placed as to have it in their power to compel many other governments of far higher spirit than theirs to turn to force for their own protection. Similarly, force and threats of force, made solely and always in support of gain-seeking and selfish advantage on the part of individuals or groups of individuals, are becoming increasingly powerful in the conduct of the life and government of civilized nations.

It is some twenty-five centuries since Moses came down from Mount Sinai bearing the Ten Commandments, of which the Sixth was THOU SHALT NOT KILL. It is twenty centuries since Jesus Christ uttered the maxim THOU SHALT LOVE THY NEIGHBOR AS THYSELF. The Christian religion, which has supposedly inspired and guided so much of western civilization, places these two principles among its foundation stones. They have also been accepted by the Jewish world and by the Moslem world as well. Therefore, they may claim the adherence in one form or another of a vast majority of the populations in the countries of Europe and America. What sign do these populations give of carrying into the practice of life and of government these fundamental principles to which they so glibly and so constantly profess adherence? No, the gap between profession and practice is wide indeed, and until it is bridged there can be no improvement in human affairs. Just so long as self-seeking, supported by threats of force, controls the policies of men within nations and of nations in their dealings with one another, just so long will the animal in man prevail over higher human nature.

In individual relationships, progress has been made to a point where, whatever regard be had for personality, no personality is sovereign. It is in each and every instance expected, and if possible required, to conform to moral law and to moral principle. This is the meaning of the organized state with its form of government and its realm of liberty.

In international relations, on the other hand, the fiction still prevails, both in law and in fact, that a nation is sovereign. It is this profoundly immoral and destructive principle which has much to do with the state of the world today. No nation is sovereign, however great, however rich or with however large a population. Moral law is sovereign, and the government of no people can refuse to accept that sovereignty without invoking the animal in man and turning back to the rule of force. When nations are collectively organized as human beings are collectively organized, and when the sovereignty of moral principle can be not only taught but, if need be, enforced by collective action, then and only then will the present reactionary, destructive and really terrifying chaos be brought to an end.

Do we wonder that men cry out day by day, "How long, O Lord, how long?"

XIX

INTERNATIONAL CO-OPERATION:
THE ONLY PATH TO PEACE

An article written for the *Légion d'Honneur Magazine*,
in honor of the 150th anniversary of the French Republic
July, 1939

INTERNATIONAL CO-OPERATION:
THE ONLY PATH TO PEACE

The practical lessons to be drawn from that process of nation-building which has been going on first in Europe and then on every other continent since the fall of the Roman Empire become plainer day by day. The prophetic forecast of King Henry IV of France, made so long ago as 1603 in his Grand Design, still points the way to that progress for which the world is waiting. Every possible attempt has been made to deal with world problems satisfactorily on the basis of a world system of independent and sovereign nations. The result has been one war after another, one reign of fear and uncertainty after another and a series of tragic steps backward following on almost every important advance in the intellectual, the economic or the political world. We now have the spectacle of nations which call themselves civilized armed to the teeth for the purpose of defense. In military language the most effective and satisfactory form of defense is quick and successful offense, but at the moment that is something which no government will publicly admit. Each insists that it is arming for defense and for defense alone.

The effect of these heavily armed nations is not only to invite, indeed to precipitate, a rule of force rather than a rule of reason but to divert from productive industry that which might vastly increase the health, the hap-

piness and the comfort of mankind to the manufacture
and maintenance of weapons of destruction on a scale
hitherto undreamt of. Moreover, the youth in each of
these lands is called upon to be trained for the use of
force without the slightest appeal to the rule of reason.
How long can such a state of affairs go on without wrecking civilization? The answer must be: Not very much
longer.

The futility of war has never been more clearly
demonstrated than by the Great War of 1914–18 and
its results. Colossal as was the destruction of human
life and human property, appalling as was the exhaust-
ing of the savings of mankind through the centuries, it
is now perfectly plain that every single end was lost for
which those allied nations which are supposed to have
won the war carried on that conflict. The nations which
were supposedly defeated at the time of Armistice Day,
November 11, 1918, and the terms of whose defeat
were recorded in the Treaties of Versailles, of the
Trianon and St.-Germain, are now in possession of everything for which they fought in the Great War and much
more besides. Are men intelligent enough to learn the
lesson which these facts teach? If they are, they will
quickly address themselves to following the only sure
path to peace, which is world organization of all civilized nations.

The statesmen of a generation ago who first conceived
the plan for a league of nations had a noble vision.
Woodrow Wilson shared that vision and gave the whole
of his great influence and authority to transforming it
into an accomplished fact. His own limitations of tem-
perament, political conditions in the United States and

the obstacles set by the allied nations in Europe, presumably victors in the war, put restrictions upon the League of Nations as established by the Treaty of Versailles which, despite brave and broad-minded administration, it has not been able to overcome. It was the intertwining of the League of Nations with the *status quo* in Europe which proved the greatest obstacle to its success. Had the Government of the United States, as so many of us urged and as both great political parties favored in their public declarations, joined in bringing about a true society of nations not linked to the *status quo* in Europe, the world would have been a very different place today. Such changes in the *status quo* as political and economic conditions have made desirable, indeed necessary, might then have been accomplished through frank and peaceful discussion under the leadership of the government of the United States, which was not an immediate party in interest. That possibility was lost through partisan folly and blindness.

Today the same call comes to the governments of the world as came in 1918–19. A way must be found to avoid any repetition of that Great War and to promote the solution of contemporary economic and political problems in peaceful terms. This can only be done by bringing into existence an organized society of nations as proposed by the American Congress by unanimous vote of both Houses in June, 1910, with the combined navies of the world as a police force to assure international security, just as the police of any great city or any country protects the peace and order of that city or that country. This is the one and only practical course to follow. Any attempt to avoid following it can only mean continuing the present rule of chaos and fear with resulting paralysis to the world's economic and political life. If war is always just below the horizon in the thought of men, it may at almost any moment rise and begin its fatal damage because of some wholly unexpected and unplanned act on the part of an individual or a group. War is not an instrument of reasonable endeavor. It is an instrument of emotional outburst with brute force and the rule of the jungle as its underlying principles.

XX

THE UNITED STATES AND HISTORY

Translation of an article written for *Le Temps*, Paris,
July 21, 1939

THE UNITED STATES AND HISTORY

It is more important today than it ever has been before that those nations in the western world which for many generations have been slowly and steadily developing a system of free government should clearly understand one another's social, economic and political methods and ideals, as well as one another's national temperaments and achievements in the fields of letters, of science and of the fine arts.

The people of the United States have this advantage over the peoples of the free nations in Western Europe: being relatively young, they take much interest in studying the history of their elders. So it happens that English and French history and literature, in particular, are carefully studied in American schools and closely followed by the American press. As a result, the people of the United States today are the best-informed people in the world. During the past two years they have been enabled to follow with particularity and an accuracy almost beyond belief every happening which has taken place in Europe, and they have been given the information which enabled them to understand not only the method of those happenings but the reasons advanced for them.

A chief need today is that American history and American literature should be studied in the schools of Great Britain and of France in order that the people of those two great nations may come to gain an understanding of the character and achievements of the people of the United States. It must not be forgotten that Thomas Jefferson, who drafted the Declaration of Independence of July 4, 1776, sat in the hall at Versailles thirteen years later when the Declaration of the Rights of Man was formulated and adopted. At that time American political thought and French political thought had many characteristics of interdependence. Not only Thomas Jefferson and Benjamin Franklin but also Lafayette were real links between two peoples then widely separated by a great ocean, a distance which has long since been overcome by the power of steam and of electricity. The co-operation of the French military forces in the War for Independence was of commanding importance and should never be forgotten. From that time to this, American political history has many valuable lessons to give to the public opinion of Great Britain and of France, and these lessons should be learned not alone by the intellectual leaders of those countries but by the great mass of their populations through study in their secondary schools and colleges.

Moreover, American literature, while by no means as extensive or as important as the literatures of Great Britain and of France, has, nevertheless, produced outstanding contributions to the intellectual life of the modern world. The essays of Ralph Waldo Emerson have long since been a classic. The poetry of Poe, of Longfellow and of Whittier is of real significance for an understanding of American life and thought. James Russell Lowell, both in prose and in verse, opened the door to a larger understanding of the American life of his time. For a long generation past, works of literary excellence in the fields of biography, of history, of economics and of politics have poured from the American press. These should be found in the libraries of Great Britain and of France and should be increasingly well known by the educated and reflective elements of the populations of those countries.

There are many different ways of waging war. Today the whole world is at war in two of these new ways—the intellectual and the economic. It is true that undeclared military war is also being waged, but much more serious are the intellectual and the economic wars. If persisted in, these two forms of conflict may readily break down all that is best and most liberal in western civilization, check, if not bring to an end, progress toward the broadening and strengthening of free institutions, and turn mankind back to another long period of rule by despots and by dictators.

In the conduct of these wars, intellectual and economic, new weapons are fashioned out of words. We are told, for example, that the largest public interest requires that war be waged upon Capitalism. But there is no such thing as Capitalism. Capital is not a principle; it is a by-product of civil and economic Liberty. Capital is what remains from the product of work after the cost of that work and the cost of the worker's maintenance have been met. Capital is therefore savings. It is not a principle but a product. It is therefore not Capital which is under attack, but Liberty, which makes Capital possible. In a free society, he who has saved some of the product of his work may use it himself or in cooperation with others, to carry on new work and to make possible new savings. All this is an essential part of civil and economic Liberty. Therefore it is that a large part of the war now under way throughout the world is being waged against Liberty.

If the free nations who have developed Liberty are to maintain their commanding position and to continue to build upon the same foundations a social, economic and political structure of increasing value to all people, they must unite together, first to understand what Liberty really means and how it finds expression, and then to act to protect and to defend it in all circumstances and against any attack from reactionary doctrines in whatever form they present themselves.

XXI

EDUCATION FOR DEMOCRACY

An address as Honorary Chairman of the
International Congress on Education for Democracy,
McMillin Academic Theatre, Columbia University,
August 15, 1939

EDUCATION FOR DEMOCRACY

To greet this distinguished and representative company drawn from so many different parts of this country and from other countries is a very high privilege. It is not often that there has been assembled for the discussion of a great public question so thoroughly representative a body, reflecting the opinion, the judgment and the experience of different types of minds and of citizenship in a half-dozen countries.

We appreciate to the full the presence here today of those distinguished representatives of Great Britain, of Poland and of other foreign lands who have been able to come across the Atlantic even at so difficult a time as that through which we are passing.

We regret that it was impossibe for the President of the French Chamber of Deputies, M. Herriot, to come to us as he had hoped and planned to do. But at the very last moment his government expressed the opinion that under conditions as they now exist it would not be wise or judicious for him to leave France. We regret his absence, but we are going to hear from him, in due time, a message of greeting and of understanding.

To those who have come to us from all parts of the United States, from every kind and type of organization interested in public affairs, I repeat this presentation of heartfelt welcome and greeting.

We have assembled here on Morningside Heights.

There could be no more suitable place in the world to discuss the far-reaching topic which is to occupy your attention. From its very beginning Columbia University has been concerned with the training and the preparation of great leaders in the building of a democratic government. Strike out from American history the name of Alexander Hamilton, of John Jay, of Robert R. Livingston, of DeWitt Clinton, all of whom were graduated from Columbia College, and how could you write the history of the making of the Federal Government of these United States?

And today our college for the training of teachers, from which sprang the initiative of this great undertaking, touches the educational life of the world in every land and at almost every point. Whether it be Australia, or South Africa, or China, or South America or any part of this Union, Teachers College has sent its influence and its inspiration to guide and shape the education of youth.

Therefore it is that here on Morningside this congress, open-minded, catholic, liberal, forward-facing, may well feel at home in an environment of understanding and appreciation.

The topic which you are to discuss and consider is the most interesting and the most important in the world of today. It transcends all topics in the field of economics and political order because it underlies them all and is fundamental to them all. Education in and for democracy, or, to turn it around, democracy guided and shaped and strengthened by education—how shall these things be done?

It is important that we should have clearly in mind

what it is that we are discussing, and therefore it is important that we define the words Education and Democracy. Both words are used very loosely, in many different senses, and are treated, therefore, in many different ways. Very frequently, the result is discussion and action which are very misleading. Therefore, it is imperative that we define for ourselves these terms.

If I were to offer my own interpretation this would be my answer: What is education? It is something very much broader and deeper than instruction of any kind, and it is something very much broader and deeper than preparation for any particular calling in life. Both instruction and vocational preparation fit into the process of education, but they are in no sense identical with it. Indeed, instruction itself is a subordinate instrument in education, since example and discipline are much more important and much more powerful. Just so vocational preparation is and can only be a subordinate part of preparation for life itself. Education, as I defined it a full generation ago, must mean a gradual adjustment to the spiritual possessions of the race, with a view to realizing one's own potentialities and to assisting in carrying forward that complex of ideas, acts and institutions which we call civilization. In other words, education in a true sense has not only to do with the individual to be educated, but with the environment into which and for which he is to be educated. The spiritual possessions of the race may be defined in many ways, but they are certainly fivefold and the child is entitled to each and all of them. He is not born into a new world, where nothing has ever happened. He is born into a world full of experience, some of the experience bitter,

some of it magnificent, and he is entitled to know what
it is about and what it means.

That inheritance is fivefold. It is scientific, it is
literary, it is esthetic, it is institutional and it is religious.
Without them all he cannot become a truly educated
or a truly cultivated man. He is entitled to know what
those who have preceded him have accomplished, what
their accomplishment means for him, and what he is to
do in the world which their accomplishment has brought
to pass.

And what is democracy? That word has almost as
many definitions as the number of those who use it. Democracy I define as government by the people in the interest of all the people, with guarantee of civil and religious liberty to every citizen. There can be no democracy
without that guarantee. Democracy is not government
by the mob. Democracy is not even government by a
majority, unless that majority respects the general welfare and puts it before individual or group interests, and
unless that majority maintains undiminished the fundamental guarantee of civil and religious liberty.

Therefore, it is imperative that each individual in
a democracy be educated to participate in carrying it
forward, to take up his duty as a citizen and neither to
shirk it nor to turn aside from it in bitterness, in dis-
satisfaction, or in antagonism.

It is literally amazing in a democracy today what a
small proportion of the possible vote is cast even in a
highly contested election. When democracy came to
Germany under the Constitution of Weimar, they broke
almost all records by casting a vote of some eighty per
cent of the possible electorate. In Parliamentary elec-

tions in Great Britain the number has frequently risen
to seventy or seventy-five per cent. Hardly anywhere
else in the world has it ever reached fifty per cent of a
possible electorate. Some years ago an analysis was
made of the vote by which the members of the Senate
of the United States as then constituted had been elected.
The highest percentage of the possible vote of his state
that any one of them had received was thirty-three,
while others received as small a percentage as seventeen,
sixteen, thirteen, twelve, ten and nine.

In other words, it is imperative that democracy be
a real democracy, that it be participated in by the whole
body of citizenship and that youth be taught that to
participate in shaping and in choosing government is
an imperative part of its life duty.

Very brief reflection upon these two definitions will
make it plain that in last resort neither education nor
democracy can rest upon brute force. Both must have
a moral foundation and be subject to intelligent appreciation.

It is in this spirit that I should counsel approaching
the specific problems of this day and hour. They cannot be waved aside by a sweep of the hand. They cannot be solved by turning to that timorous and cowardly
dictum, Wait and See. If civilization is to avoid overwhelming damage and perhaps ruin for centuries, there
is something to be done which must be done now.

Do not forget that our archæologists have been for
generations revealing to us the physical and often the
intellectual and the esthetic achievements of civilizations
long gone by, the physical remains of which are being
exhumed year by year from the sands in which centuries

of time have buried them. Plainly, these remains are representative of what were very early but nevertheless very noteworthy civilizations. Is it possible that some fate of this sort awaits our civilization? Cynics and pessimists indicate that that may be so, but the practical man of liberal mind and outlook will not yield his faith in our capacity to offer the intelligence and the courage which will avoid any such fate.

Therefore, my friends, we come to this problem, I trust, not underestimating its seriousness or its very great importance, but resolved in a spirit of confident hopefulness to find ways and means to solve it and to save the things we care for most in the world in which we live.

XXII

REPEAL THE MISCALLED NEUTRALITY ACT

Telegram to *The New York Times* in reply to
Senator Borah's speech on repeal of the Neutrality Act,
September 16, 1939

REPEAL THE MISCALLED NEUTRALITY
ACT

Senator Borah's interesting speech belongs to an age
hat is past. The world which it assumes came to its
end a generation ago. The doctrine of isolation which
t reflects is that economic nationalism which is the chief
cause of the world's troubles. It is just that doctrine
which brought on this new war and which is making
almost impossible industrial recovery in the United
States.

If we are to mind our own business we must be sure
that we know that our own business includes everything
which affects us, wherever it may be and whether it is
economic, political or intellectual. There is no longer a
distant Europe or a remote America. They are now but
a few seconds apart, and their links are many and powerful.

The present miscalled Neutrality Act puts us into this
war on the side of the aggressor. Repeal it and go back
to that neutrality which international law defines and
controls, and we shall be on sound ground.

Participation in a war does not necessarily mean mili-
ary participation. There are other ways of helping a
combatant. This miscalled Neutrality Act puts us in the
position not only of helping the aggressor but of helping those powers and influences which are the bitterest
enemies of all that we Americans hold most dear.

They are warring upon our Bill of Rights and all for which it stands in the life of man. If the neutrality of international law should operate to the advantage of those people who are fighting for the principles in which we Americans believe, well and good.

Communism and Fascism are fundamentally one, so far as their contempt for civil and religious liberty is concerned.

Let us keep out of military participation in this war, by all means; but let us not be so stupid as not to see what the war is about or how directly it affects our own interests as Americans.

XXIII

THE WORLD UPON WHICH YOUTH MUST LOOK

An address delivered at the opening of the
186th year of Columbia University,
September 27, 1939

THE WORLD UPON WHICH YOUTH
MUST LOOK

What can be said to the youth of today and tomorrow that will aid them to comprehend the world which faces them and in which they are soon to begin to do their life work? That world so far as its professed and constantly extolled ideals are concerned is in a state of well-nigh total collapse. Those principles of intellectual understanding and interpretation and those principles of morals which have for centuries been proclaimed to be the true guide of all conduct, whether personal or public, are almost everywhere lying in the dust. Their place has been taken by the most appallingly cruel and wicked manifestations of the gain-seeking motive. Modern man has returned, for the time being at least, to the jungle, where animal preys upon animal and where force and cunning, and force and cunning alone, shape the happenings day by day.

Leaving quite apart the vast intellectual and moral achievements of those civilizations which we call ancient and medieval, modern civilization has been torpedoed as by a submarine, by emotional, unintelligent and power-seeking madness. The great philosophers, men of letters and men of science who dominated the thought of the modern world during the past two hundred years are no longer recognized or even referred to as offering guidance for conduct and for public policy. Governments on at least two continents are engaged in that

type of assault, of arson and of murder which is euphe-
mistically called war.

Conditions have so developed during the past half-
century that it has now come to be within the power
of a single government not only to shape its own policies
in terms of possible war and to bend all its efforts,
economic, social and political, toward achieving success
in that war, but to compel other and otherwise-minded
governments to do the same thing in order to prevent
being demolished by force. More than this, as matters
have developed during the past twenty-five years, it is
now possible for a sufficiently dramatic and emotion-
stirring individual to gather about himself a sympathetic
and subservient group through whom he can terrorize
or hypnotize a whole people, which may be quite otherwise-minded, into a blind acquiescence in his policies.
When somewhat similar happenings took place in years
long gone by, they were attributed to an undeveloped
and far from complete civilization. They were looked
upon as something which was passing and could never
return. Today, however, as the world approaches the
middle of the twentieth century, these cruel, reactionary
and essentially barbarous forces have returned at their
very worst.

Outstanding is the example of what has happened
to the truly great German people. From the time of
Frederick the Great, that people began to take a place
of leadership in the modern world which steadily increased in importance. The great names which marked
their philosophy, their literature and their science from
the middle of the eighteenth century to the first decade
of the twentieth were quite unrivalled. German scholar-

ship, German music and German art were the center of the world's attention and approval. Today that great people has been reduced, as no great people has ever before been reduced in all history, to a position where only barbarians should be found. To suppose that the German people will permit themselves to remain forever, or even for a long time, in such a state of intellectual and moral downfall and decay is not to be believed for a moment. But if civilization is to be saved and if the forces of intelligence and morality are to be restored to even a partial but steadily growing control of public policy, the German people must not delay. Today they may have it in their power to save or to wreck the modern world. In order to save the modern world, they must first wreck the mad and reactionary tyrant who for the moment holds them in his grip. Can they and will they do it?

The most powerful appeal for perpetual peace which the literature of the world contains is that made by the outstanding German philosopher, Immanuel Kant, nearly a century and a half ago. Kant in his philosophy, in his view of life and in his appeal for a better world, represented the German mind at its highest and best. He has properly been described as the Copernicus of philosophy. He might also be described as the author of the Magna Carta of German intellectual life. If the German people of this day and generation could be brought to read Kant's immortal essay, *Zum ewigen Frieden,* and to translate its thought into action, they would quickly resume their intellectual importance in this world of ours and would lead the way toward the establishment of universal and lasting peace. To do this, however, they must free themselves from the emotional grip of an unrivalled despot whose aim is power and for whom the German people are an instrument in seeking to achieve that power. From the grip of this despot they must free themselves in order to return to the proud and commanding Germany of Herder and of Lessing, of Kant and of Fichte, of Goethe, of Heine and of Schiller, of von Ranke, of Zeller and of Paulsen, of Bach, of Beethoven, of Mendelssohn and of Wagner. They must become again the truly great German people whom the world is ready to admire and to praise. In order that all this may be possible, German slavery must give way to German freedom.

Shortly after dawn on the morning of Monday, August 3, 1914, I was alone in the great railway station at Lausanne, Switzerland. My anxious aim was to find some way to return promptly to America, since what proved to be the Great War of 1914–18 had just broken out. The French frontier was closed. The Italian frontier was closed to all but Italian citizens summoned to return to Italy for military service. I soon found that there was one other person in that great railway station besides myself. He was a railway servant more than seventy years of age and therefore not liable for that military service to which all of the younger Swiss had been called for the defense of their eastern frontier. This man was a German Swiss and viewed me, as a stranger, with unconcealed suspicion. When he found me to be an American, he spoke more freely, particularly as it was quite plain that there was no one else in that railway station to hear what he said. He told me that his two sons had been summoned by the Swiss government for the purpose of defending the Austrian frontier but that he himself, who had served in the Franco-Prussian War, was now too old to be summoned.

This railway servant then added these words, which are as remarkable as any that I have ever heard: "Sir," he said, speaking in German, "this war is not a people's war. This is a kings' war. When it is over there may not be so many kings." He doubtless lived to see Russia and Austria and Germany lose their ruling monarchs.

So, a quarter-century afterward, I may repeat in substance the words of that extraordinary man and say: "This is not a people's war. This is a despots' war, and when it is over there may not be so many despots." The conflict is between ideas and ideals. The combatants are both of German origin. They are Kant's *Zum ewigen Frieden* and Hitler's *Mein Kampf*.

XXIV

EDUCATION AND THIS CHANGING WORLD

An address delivered at the annual meetng of the
Association of Urban Universities,
Hotel New Yorker, New York,
October 24, 1939

EDUCATION AND THIS CHANGING
WORLD

Mr. President, Distinguished Guests and my Friends of this Association of Urban Universities:

Truly this is a most inspiring, as well as a most representative, gathering of American intellectual workers and leaders. You are met at a time when your calling and mine must bear a heavier responsibility than has ever before been put upon it.

This world of ours has always been a changing world. It has never stood still. Its changes have taken two very different forms. For the most part, they have been the changes of evolution, extending slowly and steadily over long centuries. Obvious causes have been at work, producing their natural ideas and results. New insights have improved the institutions which mark the social, the economic and the political life of man. Then from time to time there have been changes due to revolution. These were great changes due to the operation of forces which even now we do not fully grasp or understand. When we look back upon what man has been—among those magnificent achievements of construction which our archæologists have been uncovering in Egypt and in Mesopotamia—we are compelled to ask ourselves the question: What brought them to ruin? How did those civilizations come to an end? Why and how did those peoples and their achievements disappear from earth?

If we look back, we find ourselves face to face with

the fact that of all human institutions, education is the most powerful and the most constant—education, of which the school, the university, the laboratory and the museum are manifestations; education, the great fundamental institution of civilization, is that by which and through which man produces, understands, interprets and carries forward his outstanding achievements. Education is the institution through which and by which man collects, elaborates, applies and transmits to posterity his achievements. The school, the university, the laboratory—these are the instruments of education, that great and enduring institution with so magnificent a purpose. If education is to achieve its high purpose, it must first of all understand how it came into existence.

There have been three great forces playing upon the western world through the centuries, giving to it stimulus and ideals. The first of these forces was Jewish, which brought with it the religious feeling, the religious insight and the religious stimulation which is so abundantly recorded in the Old Testament. The next force was Greek, which gave us literature, philosophy, science and the fine arts. The third was Roman, which poured into the western world as a love of order and obedience to law, administrative efficiency and practical capacity in dealing with economic and political problems. Those three great streams of influence, religious, intellectual and practical, gave to our civilization its first understanding and the reasons for its perpetuity.

If we are to know the world of today in its changing form, and the world of tomorrow toward which it is moving, we must first make sure that we know the world of yesterday and understand the permanent forces by which it was shaped. These forces are just as likely to be revolutionary as evolutionary. No man can distinguish the one from the other until the story of history has been told and understood. Our task is to do the best we can to explain this to the youth of your world and mine.

It may be that some of you have been privileged to stand upon what seem to me to be the three most sacred and inspiring spots in the world: the summit of the Mount of Olives, the Acropolis at Athens, and the Capitoline Hill at Rome. From each and all of those three summits one looks down upon a wide expanse of territory; wide, and yet not a fraction of the size of many an American county. From each of those summits one beholds a territory on which deeds have taken place from which inspirations have gone forth that constitute the ideals of our modern belief and thought and action. And any one must be impressed, I think, with the wonderful disproportion that exists between the extent of the territory on which those scenes were enacted and the permanence and depth and sweep of their influence.

Standing on the summit of the Mount of Olives, the City of Jerusalem lies at our feet. Immediately at the foot of the hill is the garden called Gethsemane. The brook called Kedron flows between the spectator and the city wall. The great site of Solomon's Temple, now crowned by the Mosque of Omar, standing on the summit of the ancient Mount Moriah, is in the foreground. Beyond it is the hill of Zion. The town of Bethany lies at the left, and Bethlehem is just over the hills to the south. Behind are the Dead Sea and Jordan and Jericho. To the north and beyond the Damascus Gate are the hills of Samaria. Straight in front are the blue hills that run down to the Mediterranean at Jaffa. And there, all within the glance of the eye, lies this great series of historic spots that mean so much, with all their associations, for the history and civilization of the western world.

Cross the sea to the Acropolis at Athens. Go out at sunset and sit on the corner of the temple of the Wingless Victory, that most beautiful and pathetic of ruins. Immediately in front is the scene of the battle of Salamis. Beyond the hills to the right the Persians were beaten back at Marathon. In that little grove of trees yonder, in the midst of the blue fields, were the Academy of Plato and the Lyceum of Aristotle. Under the hill to the left is the theatre in which the great dramas were read to the delight of the Athenian people. Just below is Mars Hill, where the energetic voice of Paul may almost be heard thundering out, "Ye men of Athens!" Just beyond stands the very platform from which Demosthenes appealed to the Athenian people to beat back the Macedonian tyrant. There again, within one stroke of the eye, is the seat and the home of a marvellous civilization.

But two days' journey to the west is the still more familiar Capitoline Hill at Rome which looks down upon the scene of so many marvellous events, the homes of so many extraordinary men, all of whom live and move today in our literature and our life. Now compare for one moment the narrow territory on which those historic scenes were enacted; consider the smallness of the spring from which those great and perennial streams have come, and then look out upon the great field of our modern opportunity. Compare those scenes with this broad land of ours stretching from ocean to ocean and almost from the frost line on the north to the Gulf on the south, with its one hundred and twenty millions of people, its diversified soil, and every opportunity for achievement, exaltation and development. Contrast the feeble beginnings, geographically speaking, of our civilization; contrast them with the opportunities that are in the hands of this modern, highly cultivated, highly differentiated and developed people; and then ask yourself the question: What are the responsibilities resting upon education?

Moreover, we must always take full account of personality. One of the most extraordinary happenings in the history of mankind is the influence over generations of people of a great, outstanding personality. Such personalities have exercised enormous influence over the minds of masses of the people, playing upon those minds, rousing them into action often foolish and wicked, and stimulating their emotions until the bubble bursts. We have seen it all time and time again. We had supposed that the development of Europe and the development of America, with its free institutions, were secure. No sooner had this seemed plain than the amazing despot, Napoleon, took practical command of the continent of, Europe. By sheer force he reordered and changed the whole course of its development for a generation. Napoleon's control came to an end, but the lesson which it taught is still with us.

What we are facing today is another and very similar outburst of that emotional leadership over the masses exercised through force and threat of force, after the world had just passed through what seemed like con-

structive progress in every field of human effort and
human power. Literature and the fine arts, scientific
advance, industry and commerce, were all going forward
in what we expected would remain a peaceful and an
orderly world. Today we are face to face with another
demonstration of the power which a captain of the emotions may possess, endangering a whole generation of
mankind and many peoples other than his own. There
is where we are at the present moment. We face not
only one or more of these great personalities in other
lands, but also the attempt of many lesser personalities
in our own land to check the progress of man and to
shake the foundations upon which that progress has
rested. These personalities offer a challenge to our
social, economic and political methods, convictions and
ideals. We Americans are inheritors of all that is best
in the western world. We have been developed under
the influence of the great Jewish tradition, the great
Greek tradition and the great Roman tradition of which
I have spoken. We have achieved liberty under the
law. This means the right of private property, the state,
the church, freedom of the press and of speech, each and
all of which are fundamental to man's progress as we
conceive it.

What can an American say, as he faces this changing
world, more proudly and justly, than:

> My country, 'tis of thee,
> Sweet land of liberty,
> Of thee I sing.

XXV

THE PROBLEM BEFORE ENGLAND AND AMERICA

An address delivered at the dinner given by The Pilgrims
of the United States in honor of the Marquess of Lothian,
Plaza Hotel, New York,
October 25, 1939

THE PROBLEM BEFORE ENGLAND
AND AMERICA

Your Excellency, Your Excellencies and our Distinguished Guests, my Fellow Pilgrims: This evening, we offer hearty and affectionate welcome not only to a newly designated Ambassador from Great Britain, but to a statesman who will find in these United States a host of warm and admiring friends. No other Ambassador, save only James Bryce, has ever come to America having like familiarity with our people, our institutions and our national ideals.

The government of Great Britain could have made no happier choice at this troubled and indeed most dangerous time in modern history than that of the Marquess of Lothian. He comes equipped with that scholarship, with that experience and with that international understanding which are at this moment absolutely invaluable. He comes in the spirit of that fine declaration by Cecil Rhodes, whose trust Lord Lothian has administered through so many years, that he hoped that those who were to profit by the international scholarships which he was about to endow would form an attachment to the country where they went for study without in any wise weakening their affection for the land of their birth.

The nations of the earth are now sharply divided, almost unconsciously and despite their legal and formal equality of status, into the great and the small. They are also divided, regardless of their size or their power, into those where a free public opinion guides and rules government and those in which there is no public opinion to serve this purpose.

These facts gravely affect the service of an ambassador and directly indicate how that service may best be performed. Between nations in which free public opinion exists and eventually dominates public policy, the most successful ambassador in this twentieth century will be one who becomes ambassador not only to a government but to a people. If an ambassador confines his activities to formal relations with the department of foreign affairs of the government to which he is accredited, he may miss a great part of his opportunity for the highest type of public service to his own people. If, on the other hand, he finds ways and means to enter freely and intimately into the unofficial life of the people to whose government he is accredited, he not only will strengthen himself as ambassador, but also will find ways and means better to understand the people with whom he is living and better to interpret the institutions and ideals of the people whose representative he is.

In other words, between countries in which public opinion rules, an ambassador performs but a part, and indeed a very small part, of his service, if he confines himself to the official routine of his great office. If, on the other hand, through travel, through contact with organizations and groups of different kinds and interests, scattered all over the country, he comes really in contact with the people as a whole, his own importance as ambassador is greatly increased and the links between his own land and that where he officially dwells are multiplied and strengthened many times. This means that the twentieth-century ambassador from a country in which public opinion rules to another country in which public opinion rules is in a unique position of influence and of opportunity.

It is commonplace to say that the world of today is strangely perplexed, as it watches through its abundant channels of information what takes place day by day and almost hour by hour. It seeks to find a meaning for it all. What can that meaning be? There is a famous chapter in Gibbon's *History of the Decline and Fall of the Roman Empire* in which he points out that in the age of the Antonines, the union and internal prosperity of the Roman people were almost complete and ideal. Men were at peace; they were prosperous, and they were happy. Literature and philosophy flourished, and life seemed to go forward with satisfaction and content. The great cities of the Roman Empire were connected with one another and with Rome by public highways which traversed the entire empire. One great chain of communication from the northwest to the southeast point of that empire extended over four thousand and eighty Roman miles. Agriculture, which is the foundation of manufacture, was prosperous, and contentment was obvious everywhere.

Nevertheless, Rome was soon to break and fall. Why? Because what Gibbon describes as a "slow and secret poison" was introduced into the vitals of the Roman Empire. The minds of men were gradually reduced to the same level, and the fire of genius was extinguished. Men were accepting laws and government from the will of their sovereign, and what had been a vigorous and

independent and intellectual life became one dominate
with increasing completeness by the will of a dictator

Must this modern world, looking back over nearl
two thousand years to the age of the Antonines, con
template a fate similar to that of Rome? Is it possible-
after all that the intervening centuries have accomplishe
in works of the mind, in an expansion of science whic
is truly revolutionary, in the application of our nev
knowledge to every form and aspect of human life an
human undertaking, and with the barriers of distanc
removed by the electric spark, with leagues reduced t
millimeters and months to seconds of time—is it possibl
that modern man cannot continue his forward march an
avoid the dreadful fate which attended the leaders o
civilization so long ago?

The story of what has happened since ancient Rom
fell is a long and complicated one but, as we estimate an
measure progress, it is a story of what seems like steady
advance in the major activities of man. We have pro
duced no Plato and no Aristotle, and the great work
of Greek and Roman sculpture remain in their place o
commanding excellence, but in almost every other department of life and activity we have been marching
as we think, forward, for centuries.

Nevertheless, the essential elements of the human
problem remain the same as they have always been.
These are, for man himself, whether the spirit of service
shall or shall not be subordinate to the gain-seeking
instinct. For the organized social and political order,
the problem is whether government shall be the creature
and the servant of men or whether men shall be the
dependent and obedient servants of government. Here

re the two everlasting battles on the field of human
fe. We make progress when the one side wins; we go
ackward when the other side takes command for a
onger or a shorter time.

The unbridled gain-seeking impulse, whether indi-
idual, social or political, can achieve its ends only by
ne rule of force. Likewise, government can take over
nd express the individual human being only by the
ule of force. The rule of force means war. It may
egin with economic, with social and with political force,
ut ultimately it will surely take the form of military
orce and of armed war for the purpose of defending
nd upholding itself. No matter what uniform it may
wear, its aims and its methods are always the same.

It has been the happy fortune of the English-speaking
eoples and those who have come under their influence
o have marched farther forward along the path toward
stablishing the rule of reason over the rule of force
nan any other peoples in the world. There are reasons
or this which go far back into the history of our race.
The instinct of individual initiative, individual action
nd individual accomplishment rather than group or
ational organization and action began to show itself first
n the life of our Anglo-Saxon forebears. The march
orward of these ideas and ideals was slow and difficult.
There were many burdens to bear and many obstacles
o be removed, but from the time of Magna Carta down
nrough the Petition of Rights, the Bill of Rights, the
ederal Constitution of the United States with its Bill
f Rights, and the subsequent increasingly liberal legis-
ation of the British Empire, these ideas and ideals have
een carried forward until we felt justified in taking it

for granted that they were secure for all time and safe
from serious attack.

We are now learning to our dismay that this is not
the case and that they are neither secure nor safe from
serious attack, either within or without our nations.
Within the populations of these English-speaking countries, there are voices raised to tell us that we are on the
wrong track and what we need is regimentation, discipline, a powerful governing force rather than individual initiative and individual skill and individual accomplishment. In other words, we are told that discipline
is better than freedom, that government is superior to
the individual citizen, and that all that we have been
doing for centuries has led only to futile and harmful
results.

Strange as it may seem, those who preach these amazing doctrines really seem to believe them. They really
seem to prefer the rule of force to the rule of reason,
regimentation to opportunity, uniformity to excellence.
When we look outside our own borders, we find whole
peoples, numbered by the tens of millions, holding in
one form or another precisely these views. What we
are looking out upon today is the determined effort of
these wholly reactionary doctrines, as I believe them to
be, to establish themselves throughout the world by the
rule of force.

If, by any chance, what I have been saying represents
the actual happenings in this twentieth-century world,
then surely we had better turn back to the pages of Gibbon and see whether we cannot learn from the experience
of Rome how the fate of Rome may be avoided. In my
judgment, this is the present-day task of the English-

speaking peoples. They must more fully understand themselves and each other. They must more completely gain knowledge of the experience of every member of the English-speaking race, in whatever hemisphere or on whatever continent. They must learn how their fundamental principles have most successfully manifested themselves, and just what dangers and temptations they must be able to avoid. There are lessons to be learned in the motherland, Great Britain itself, in Australia, in Canada and even in a dozen smaller colonies and islands whose administrative experience has much to teach.

Surely, a situation such as this offers unrivalled opportunity to an ambassador from Great Britain to the United States, as well as to an ambassador from the United States to Great Britain. Here are stupendous problems to be studied and, if possible, to be solved. Here are scores of happenings to be understood and to be interpreted. What equipment for this task can be better than that which includes the best of academic training at Birmingham and at Oxford, long experience in the administration of public business in Great Britain, in India and in South Africa, and particularly in the administration of the Rhodes Trust over a generation?

It is because he is equipped with this magnificent endowment of natural ability, of public experience and of the highest ideals, that we repeat our heartfelt and affectionate welcome to the Marquess of Lothian as he undertakes his great task as Ambassador of Great Britain at Washington!

XXVI

THE PROBLEM OF WAR

Talks to Students

TALKS TO STUDENTS

Second Series
on invitation of the editors of
The Columbia *Spectator*
October and November, 1939

THE PROBLEM OF WAR

Those who, like myself, have for forty years past made every possible effort to prevent war by removing the causes of war are staggered by the happenings which now absorb the world's attention. It would seem incredible, after all that has been said and done regarding war and its causes and after the shocking experiences which attended the Great War of 1914–18, that still another war or series of wars of world-wide proportions should be under way.

It is usual to speak of a European war and then for many to add that such a war can be no concern of ours. But there is no European war. There is world-wide war, centered at present in Europe, with repercussions in Asia and in Africa. This war is fundamentally economic, financial and political, and needs but little urging to take on military form. The present war, which began by being economic and political, has now taken on that military form, the results of which no one is wise enough to forecast. Were the peoples of the world to be questioned, they would with substantial unanimity say that they are opposed to war and earnestly in favor of preventing war through removing the causes of war. Nevertheless, absolutely nothing is being done by governments to prevent war by removing the causes of war.

There are those in this land and in other lands who insist that what is going on away from our own doorstep can be no concern of ours. Put bluntly, that can only mean that they have neither understanding of what is going on nor any real sense of moral responsibility for the welfare of their fellow men. A very large proportion of those who emotionally agitate and exclaim for peace are in reality for war, if judged by the course of action which they would make possible. That course of action which they urge leads straight to war. If men could be persuaded to leave off agitating for peace in purely rhetorical and emotional terms, and tackle the real problem of preventing war by removing the causes of war, there would still be time to save our civilization from the fate which seems to threaten it.

So far as the people of the United States are concerned, they are on record again and again during the past thirty years in favor of taking the lead in organizing the nations of the world effectively to prevent war by removing the causes of war. In June, 1910, the Congress of the United States by unanimous vote of both houses—no Republican and no Democrat dissenting—supported this policy. Following the Great War, both political parties declared for precisely this course of action in their platforms of 1920, and both candidates for the presidency in that year publicly and unqualifiedly supported it.

Why has nothing been done? This is the real question for Americans to answer, since their responsibility for the present tragic state of affairs is direct and overwhelming. Their declarations have been perfect, but the action of their government has been nonexistent.

OUR NATIONAL OPPORTUNITY

It should now be obvious to every one that the military war which has already completely disrupted our international trade and which is certain to have an increasingly damaging effect upon our agriculture, our industry and our transportation, may soon take on a form which will shock and horrify the whole world.

War was certainly bad enough when it was a contest between specially organized military and naval forces, and when those who directly participated in it were almost the only sufferers. Under present-day conditions, however, the barbaric cruelty and destruction of war quickly reach vast numbers of innocent nonparticipants. Travelers by sea are blown into the ocean without notice, and left to save themselves if that be possible. Women and children who have nothing more to do with the war than they have with the planet Mars are exposed to tragic attacks from the air by bombs and by poison gas.

If we had read of all this in the history of an ancient people, we should have looked upon it as an accompaniment of early barbarism. We should have rejoiced that in our advanced state of civilization no such happenings were possible. Yet here are these very happenings! Our news is crowded with the record of them not only day by day but hour by hour.

What are we Americans going to do about it?

We may, of course, if we are sufficiently unintelligent and sufficiently cowardly, merely sit still and deplore it all. We may wring our hands and express our deep regret that such things as these could still happen in our modern world. Nevertheless, the question presses for answer—What are we going to do about it?

The most inadequate of answers is that we Americans are neutral and therefore need do nothing whatever about it. If that were proposed as an explanation of why one did nothing when he saw women and children who did not live in the same house being burned and tortured by fire, or a passer-by of whom he had no knowledge being assaulted by a bandit within plain sight, we should have but one comment to make, and that comment would not be very flattering. It is precisely this same comment which is called for if we sit still and watch assault, arson and murder on a huge national and international scale and do nothing about it.

The power of the American people is immense. They have demonstrated over a period of one hundred and fifty years their ability to deal with almost every difficult problem of organized government and of national conduct and policy. Their present population, while dominantly of English-speaking origin, is drawn from every civilized nation in the world, and each one of these elements has been made welcome in the United States. Each one has contributed its part to our national well-being and our national influence. What use are we going to make of that well-being and that influence? If we were obliged to find our answer in the proceedings of the United States Senate as printed day by day in *The Congressional Record,* we should have to say that it would be such an answer as the super-verbose and the dimly lighted might be expected to give. Is it possible that we Americans cannot do better than that? Believe me, the whole world is waiting for an answer to this question.

THE FIRST STEP FORWARD

If the government of the United States were to recognize its moral obligation to bring this most dangerous of all wars to a quick end, what could it, representing a noncombatant nation, undertake to do? The answer is that it is not now too late to do what it could and should have done months ago. That is to direct the attention of the governments of combatant peoples to the fact that they are under obligation to the government and people of the United States to renounce war as an instrument of national policy and to undertake the settlement of international differences and disputes through conference, through arbitration or through judicial process.

Since this obligation to the government and people of the United States has obviously not been met, we have a direct and definite moral interest in knowing why it has not been met and why it cannot be met even now. If formal international pledges and obligations are to mean nothing, what can be the use of treaties? In such case, what can prevent the quick and complete return of this modern world to the persistent and permanent rule of force, a characteristic of the jungle which had been thought to be displaced in this twentieth century?

The international obligation of more than sixty governments to renounce war as an instrument of national policy was made in the Pact of Paris, first proposed by

Monsieur Briand to the government of the United
States on April 6, 1927. It was finally accepted and
signed by fifteen nations on August 27, 1928, and afterward subscribed to by nearly fifty governments more.
It is true that the ink of these signatures to the Pact of
Paris was hardly dry before many of these governments,
including the greatest and the strongest, began to arm
for war on land, at sea and in the air. The result is
spread out before the whole world.

Following the Pact of Paris, there has developed a
new technique in the conduct of aggressive war which
is of more than passing interest. Japan did not declare
war when it invaded and attacked China and the Chinese
people. Italy did not declare war when it entered
Ethiopia, drove its monarch from the country, over-
turned its government and took control of the territory
and its population. Germany did not declare war when
it started so skillfully the absorption first of Austria, then
of Czechoslovakia and then of Poland, and cast eager
eyes on other neighboring peoples both to the east and to
the west. Therefore these nations would probably be
bold enough to say that they were not violating the Pact
of Paris but only preserving the peace and preventing
wicked injustices to those fellow nationals who might
happen to live under the jurisdiction of other and separate governments. England and France did not declare
an aggressive war on Germany, and no war has been
declared on Russia. England and France simply said
that under their obligation to Poland, since Poland had
been attacked by an aggressor, a state of war existed
between themselves and that aggressor.

It would clarify matters mightily if the government

of the United States should press these facts upon the attention of the public opinion of the world, and insist upon having some answer and some explanation as to how it happens that a definite public obligation to the government and people of the United States has been so ruthlessly discarded and violated. The answers would make interesting reading and would point the way to the next step to be taken.

WHAT MIGHT HAPPEN NEXT

Were the government of the United States to ask of each combatant nation why it is acting in violation of the terms of the Pact of Paris, to which the government of the United States is a party, a very interesting situation might quickly present itself. The answers would be either excuses or explanations, or something of both. Whatever form they took, they would open the way for the government of the United States to propose to the governments of the other signatories to the Pact of Paris which were themselves noncombatant, to press upon the governments of the combatant nations a definite proposal for armistice pending an international consultation as to how the present military operations might be brought to an end and the terms of the Pact of Paris complied with. The people of every one of the countries which are now formally or informally at war would be only too glad to avoid the horrible destruction and loss which continuance of hostilities must involve. Therefore great pressure would be brought upon the governments of the combatant nations by their own people to act upon such an invitation.

A real difficulty, however, would arise from the fact that in the case of at least two of the combatant nations their present governments so control all forms of publicity that it would not be easy to have knowledge of this invitation reach those populations. On the other hand, ways might be found to overcome that obstacle. Were this invitation accepted, however grudgingly, the government of the United States would be on the sound ground which it took for itself in the joint resolution passed by the Congress in June, 1910, to which reference has already been made.

It would be becoming that the proposed conference should be held at Geneva. There a real beginning was made, following the Great War of 1914–18, in organizing the world for the establishment and protection of peace. For reasons which are now pretty clearly understood, that undertaking fell far short of accomplishing all that was expected of it. It has, however, accomplished a great deal and is still doing so, in fields of activity other than the political. It is astonishing how little of this is known by the American people. The issue of *International Conciliation* for September, 1939, published by the Carnegie Endowment for International Peace, copies of which may be had for the asking, records in full detail the co-operation of the United States in dealing with problems of world organization. The list of undertakings and achievements is long and impressive.

With representatives of the nations of the world once seated around a council table under the leadership of the government of the United States, itself the representative of a peace-loving and a peace-supporting people, it might not be long before the world outlook would be very different from that which it now is. Whether that be the result or not, surely the attempt is worth making. The alternative is almost too terrible to contemplate.

Were such a conference to be held in the near future, what topics should the government of the United States press for consideration?

WORLD ECONOMIC ORGANIZATION

It is probable that the chances of making progress at a world conference in the near future would be much improved were questions of territorial readjustment and colonies—however pressing they may seem to be at the moment—postponed until there had been an attempt at agreement upon some economic policies which must certainly be established if prosperity and peace are to return to the world. Should these policies be established, it would then be possible to approach, in a quite different spirit from that which is now practicable, questions involving the readjustment of national boundaries, the treatment of minorities and the reassignment of colonies and mandates. Should these questions be placed first upon the agenda, it might not be possible to make any progress whatever.

Another great practical advantage in undertaking first the study of international economic organization is the fact that a program for such organization has been proposed on highest authority at a time when the world was not at war and when these economic problems could be approached without temper or passion. This program

is that agreed upon by the international conference held
at Chatham House, London, in March, 1935, on the
invitation of the Carnegie Endowment for International
Peace. The members of this conference—sixty-two in
number, coming from ten different countries—included
many of the most distinguished men in the world.
Among them were statesmen of large experience, men
of affairs, diplomats of long service and men holding
most responsible positions in the financial administration
of their several countries: Belgium, Canada, France,
Germany, Great Britain, Holland, Italy, Norway, Sweden and the United States. The astonishing thing
is that the recommendations of this conference were
adopted by unanimous vote. Had such action been predicted in advance, it would have seemed wholly imprac-
ticable and quite preposterous; but the action was taken
by this outstanding company of representative men from
ten nations. Moreover, the International Chamber of
Commerce, which represents the men of affairs in every
land and which is without any political relationship or
bias, unanimously approved this program a few months
after it had been agreed upon.

Plainly, then, material is ready for immediate consideration by such an international conference as is suggested without wasting any time whatsoever on pre-
liminary discussions or the work of numerous commit-
tees. If the conference were practically minded, it could
get down to business at once. By pursuing this course
and by postponing, until these economic questions had
been answered, all matters relating to the readjustment
of national boundaries and colonies, it might prove practicable to make genuine progress in bringing this war

to an end before it has wholly ruined the trade and commerce of the world, wasted the world's savings and discouraged the entire human race as it has never been discouraged before.

A CONSTRUCTIVE PROGRAM

The constructive program to be submitted to an international conference should have as its direct and immediate aim the restoration of confidence to a world in which confidence has been wholly destroyed. Solemn treaties now mean nothing, and the public declarations of leaders of opinion have time and again in these recent years been promptly contradicted by their acts. If confidence is to be restored, the rule of moral principle must first be restored. Falsehood, trickery and threats of force must abdicate or be sent to concentration camps.

As the Conference at Chatham House makes clear, if confidence is to be restored there must be first of all promotion of trade and reduction of unemployment, stabilization of national monetary systems and better organization of the family of nations to give security and to strengthen the foundations on which international peace must rest. As the Conference at Chatham House pointed out, since it is the commercial policy of creditor nations which is of supreme moment to the financial and economic stability of debtor countries in all parts of the world, it is of vital importance that the governments of the United States and of Great Britain, the world's two greatest creditor nations, take the lead in immediate action, in co-operation with other governments, to the end that measures may be agreed upon that will enable the debtor nations to meet their obligations in goods and services. This step alone would be of material assistance in the work of creating stability and restoring confidence.

Next, the existing tariff policies must be revised in the broad-minded and liberal fashion in which, under the leadership of Secretary Hull, the government of the United States is now proceeding to multiply reciprocal arrangements with other nations to the end that international trade be developed and increased and the prosperity of all the co-operating countries greatly advanced. The world is faced with every possible difficulty, natural and artificial, in carrying on international trade and in securing stable employment for its population. Exchange restrictions, quotas and high tariffs are the obstacles to be overcome. The accumulation of gold in a few centers and the hoarding of gold on a huge scale are as harmful as possible to the development of international trade relations.

Even today it might be possible for the governments of France, Great Britain and the United States to take joint action for the purpose of coming to a provisional stabilization of exchange on the basis of gold, with a view to the establishment of a stable world gold standard which might shortly become universal in its acceptance and its influence.

The fact of the matter is that the present war is at bottom an economic war. It is being carried on largely by economic means and to achieve specific economic ends. If a nation's industry and agriculture can be exhausted and if its population can be prevented from securing adequate food supplies, a war can be won in the field of economics without the huge slaughter involved in a war which is waged wholly by military and naval forces. It is because this is fundamentally an economic war that the peace which we seek must be fundamentally and primarily an economic peace. If economic peace be gained, then all talk of encirclement becomes meaningless. No nation can be described as encircled which has free and unrestricted trade and monetary relations with its neighbors far and near. It is this fundamental and many-sided economic problem which must first be solved if peace is to return.

TIME PRESSES

If the repeated declarations of American policy to take part, and a leading part, in the reconstruction of a broken world are to be made effective, there is no time to be lost. These declarations are constant and continuing from President McKinley's noteworthy statement made at Buffalo, New York, on September 5, 1901, the day before his life was ended by an assassin, until the present confusion of thought and policy, both at Washington and in the country at large, was brought about as a result of the pathetic political quarrels and animosities which centered around the personality of President Wilson.

Clear thinking and moral purpose require that the American people put that sort of unworthy and demoralizing political warfare behind them and give their attention to principles and to ideals. We Americans are harassed in our public life by a very large and busy group of office-seekers and office-holders who are concerned not with the public interest or with fundamental principles of government, but simply with supporting or attacking an outstanding personality who may happen at the moment to be the holder of high public office or a candidate for it. All that is as unbecoming to the American people as it is disastrous to their national interests.

The present-day world is being shaken to its foundations. The war now being waged in Europe is in no proper sense of the term a purely European war. It must be repeated that what is taking place is a world-wide war, with the center of its military contests on the continent of Europe and in European waters. When and how those military contests will spread, and what other nations they will invade and involve, no man is wise enough to foresee.

This is the moment for the government of the United States to act in accordance with the famous joint resolution passed by the Congress—I again repeat, by unanimous vote of both Houses—in June, 1910. Twenty-nine years ago, the answer made by the governments of Great Britain, of France, of Germany and of Austria when this joint resolution was presented to them, was, "Wait and See." The world waited, and now there is no one so blind that he cannot see.

XXVII

THE FAMILY OF NATIONS, 1939

An address delivered over the Columbia Broadcasting Network, New York, Armistice Day, November 11, 1939 with addresses by Sr. Oswaldo Aranha, Minister of Foreign Relations, Rio de Janeiro; Doctor Gabriel Turbay, Ambassador of Colombia, Washington; Doctor Hu Shih, Ambassador of China, Washington; Doctor Antonio Sánchez de Bustamente y Sirvén, Judge of the Permanent Court of International Justice, Habana; Doctor Juan Demóstenes Arosemena, President of Panamá.

THE FAMILY OF NATIONS, 1939

We may easily forgive those who think it strange that in the presence of today's world happenings we again pause to celebrate Armistice Day. There is just now less of anything which could be described as an armistice than has ever before been recorded in the world's history. Not only are military, naval and air arms in active and destructive use both on land and on sea, but the cruel and merciless results of that use make the world aghast. The amazing thing is that these military, naval and air attacks, so frightening and so destructive, are being organized and carried on in defiance of the public opinion of every civilized people and against their deeper will.

Why is it then that governing groups or individuals in two or three nations have been able to frighten the world into war and, as seen from the surface of things, have been able to count upon the support of their own populations in so doing? At the moment this is the central point of the whole discussion of war and peace. Why, if these populations do not wish to fight, if the mothers do not wish to sacrifice their husbands and their sons, if those engaged in agriculture and in industry, in commerce and in finance, are fearful at the thought of the destruction of all that upon which their livelihood and their life-interest rest, why is it that these international wars can still be projected, organized and carried on?

The answer is that it is done by sheer emotion, by building barriers to reflection and contemplation and by sweeping toward their own destruction vast masses of people in spite of the fact that their first real concern is for safety and happiness. In the case of those countries where public opinion rules and in which government rests upon that public opinion, this task of overcoming reason by emotion must always be much more difficult than in the case of those countries where public opinion has been either subjected to persecuting regimentation or entirely stamped out. It would doubtless be quite impossible in this day and generation for a democracy in which public opinion ruled to be involved by its government in an aggressive war. Such a democracy must, however, be prepared for defense in case of attack, unless democracy is to be crushed out by despotism in some one of its many forms.

Therefore what we have to try to understand and to explain is the power of the despot to lead, indeed to compel, his people to follow him into an aggressive course of action against a neighboring nation in spite of the strong preference of his fellow countrymen for peace and prosperity. At various times in the history of the world, including the history of this modern world, we have seen illustration after illustration of the power of the emotional appeal to public sentiment and to public action if only that appeal could find some real or supposed grievance to serve as its basis. This means that one must look back a little through the years gone by to find even a partial explanation for the power of an emotional leader over any modern people, particularly one which has reached an exceptional height of intellectual development. In order that this emotional appeal may be effective, it must turn to some grievance, some injury, some injustice, some cruelty, in times not long past, in order to get the response which it seeks.

We in the United States have seen the power of these emotional and unreasoning appeals from time to time in matters of domestic policy. We have seen them exercise influence for perhaps a decade and then finally yield to the constructive power of reflection and better understanding. The world does not yet seem to have reached a point where similar experiences may be expected in the life of nations in regard to their dealings with one another.

We are told that the obstacle to a wiser and more moral relationship between governments is patriotism. May it not be that this is what Doctor Johnson meant when he used that much quoted and much attacked sentence: "Patriotism is the last refuge of a scoundrel"? In recording this statement, Boswell goes on to say that Doctor Johnson did not mean a real and generous love of country, but that pretended patriotism which so many in all ages and countries have made a cloak for self-interest. Perhaps Doctor Johnson in his extreme language put his finger upon a deep truth. Perhaps it is the case that what may be described as blind and passionate love of country, instead of thoughtful and intelligent appreciation of a country's underlying institutions and ruling ideals, is that which rouses mass emotion to undertake armed conflict. If that be true, then our task must be to teach true patriotism. This in turn would mean love of country and devotion to it as a true instrument of civilization, as a power in advancing the moral ideals and in caring for the welfare and protection of our country's neighbors, instead merely of our country itself.

We come back therefore to the old, old story. It is self-interest fighting the spirit of service; it is selfishness blocking the road to human kindliness, human co-operation and human accomplishment. Truly there is nothing new about all this, but we must not lose our courage or our hope as we go forward to deal with this age-old problem in terms of today and tomorrow.

I now have the pleasure of presenting a distinguished statesman from Brazil, one who has held high office in his country—Minister of Justice, then Minister of Finance, who for four years was Ambassador to the United States and is now Minister of Foreign Relations. I present to you Oswaldo Aranha, Minister of Foreign Relations of Brazil. We take you now to Rio de Janeiro—

Sr. Aranha: By accepting the invitation to participate in this broadcast designed to commemorate Armistice Day, I wished to pay a warm tribute of admiration to President Nicholas Murray Butler, the uncompromising champion of all noble causes, to whom nothing human is foreign, and who has been in this last quarter of a century a source of lasting spiritual influence to his country and to the world. I wished also to express the appreciation of my country and mine of the work done by the Carnegie Endowment for International Peace, whose notable services to world-wide peace education and to international understanding and good will deserve the highest praise from all public-minded persons.

Twenty-one years ago today, a large portion of civilized mankind was coming to the end of a long-protracted and cruel war, during which a huge amount of material wealth was destroyed and millions of lives were wrecked forever, leaving deep wounds which only time could heal. But, despite that tremendous accumulation of ruins, a great hope was entertained by many men and women in every country that an enduring peace could at last be found.

That hope failed lamentably, and that failure overshadows the celebration of today and darkens the whole future of mankind. The same generation which had then known the horror of the war is now again in the throe of another great war, involving some among the leading countries of western civilization, a war which may prove to have a far-reaching influence upon the fate of the civilized world.

Yet war is not an inevitable fact nor a general law of life as a certain conception of moral Darwinism pretends, but rather a remaining trace of primitive life.

In the early society the relations between social groups were governed by struggle. But human consciousness has evolved through different phases until it reached its present stage of spiritual and moral development. The primitive man saw in war the possibility of proving the superiority of his gods over the gods of the other tribes. War was clearly the result of that animistic conception of life peculiar to our ancestors. It is true that the animals live on prey, that they subsist by attack and defense, but animals do not make war.

They feel no exultation when victorious nor humiliation when defeated.

War is thus a human fact corresponding to a remote age of the evolution of consciousness. War is against life, whose main characteristic is self-enjoyment, creative activity and purposes. War is the negation of the spirit, that restless reality which is ever creating itself. It was the stress on biological facts which has brought about the theories pretending to justify war.

As to its practical results, war is entirely negative. It exalts men only to throw them into the worst forms of savagery. A man who lives only to defend himself ceases to be a creative mind, almost ceases to be a man. Likewise, the human society, in order not to lose its humanity and to avoid decay, must put an end to the struggle which divides itself internally and accept in the external relations the rule of law.

Wars still recur because statesmen still make use of them as means to solve their problems. Hence the belief in the inevitability of war, a notion which, although false, has done much to entertain in the states an attitude of war preparedness, which tends to make war really inevitable.

How different is the situation in America! The civilization in this continent was from its beginning an adventure in the realm of co-operation. Men coming from other continents soon found that, in order to overcome the obstacles set in their way to the conquest of the new lands, they were compelled to help each other in every respect, morally and materially, and so began that long experience in co-operation from which Pan Americanism was born. War, thank God, was never an instrument of policy in the blessed land of America. Our development and progress were the result of persuasion, of the ever-increasing application of technique to the forces of nature, thus making them servants instead of enemies. The vigor of our peoples has been preserved by the widespread sense that high aims are worth while. Hence the idealism that pervades our life. From the century-old struggles of Europe, we learned the lesson that, every time nations or individuals strove to isolate themselves, the result was impoverishment and decay. Thus, we always viewed mankind as one man who never dies, and that vision strengthened in us the sentiment of growth and union. We never lost sight of the fact that peaceful relations between individuals as between nations create in the minds a new feeling of humanity which the ancient civilization ignored. By thinking and acting in this manner, under the pressure of social needs and of wills ever more conscious of the spiritual solidarity, we created in America a society of nations based not only on economical and political interests but on a consciousness of international solidarity.

Of the vitality of this conception we had only a few days ago a remarkable proof in Panamá. There the twenty-one republics of this hemisphere asserted their will to co-operate, to maintain their sacred union, and, in face of a major war in Europe, which they deplore, their firm intention to preserve the ideals which are essential to American civilization. In the days of gloom through which the world is passing, this Panamá gathering was a ray of hope.

One of the greatest attainments of that conference was undoubtedly the declaration of a safety zone around the

continent. Threatened by the consequences of a war of
great magnitude in Europe and Asia, the American republics formulated a new conception which is indeed ex-
istential because it represents, in the last analysis, the
affirmation by America of its right to remain true to
itself and free from interference of belligerent activities
in its life.

In the tragedy that overcame Europe and Asia, the
role of America is to remain united and strong, ready to
exercise its moral influence over the peoples involved in
war, in order that peace may again be with them.
Nothing could be worthier of this continent. The true
feature of America is to yearn for things which are not
yet, for the future, for progress. And peace is the thing
most desired by all.

ANNOUNCER: We return you to New York—

DOCTOR BUTLER: We shall next have the pleasure
of hearing from a distinguished South American diplo-
mat, the Ambassador of the Republic of Colombia at
Washington, formerly Prime Minister of his country
and its diplomatic representative in Belgium, in Perú,
in Italy and in Switzerland; Chief of the Colombian
Delegation at the League of Nations, 1935-37; Minister of Foreign Affairs in 1938, President of the Senate
in 1939; and last month appointed Ambassador to the
United States. I have the honor to present Doctor
Gabriel Turbay, Ambassador of Colombia, who speaks
to you from Washington—

DOCTOR TURBAY: Today, Armistice Day, the world

is engaged in war. We cannot say that we are celebrating the suspension of hostilities that awakened such great joy twenty-one years ago. After four years of war, misery and devastation, the voice of an American idealist was heard inviting the nations of the world to make peace. Arms were laid down with the hope that the peace of the nations of the world might be preserved upon a juridical basis making impossible resort to the use of force in international relations. The Treaty of Versailles wanted to give expression to the desire of the people to live in peace. However, it did not achieve that purpose, as the present European war proves, nor did it prevent the long period of agitation and violence in international relations through which the world has been living for the past five years. I do not pretend to point out the causes of the failure. I wish to observe only that the nature of the Treaty of Versailles, upon which the Covenant of the League of Nations was based, undermined its very existence. The spirit of Versailles was necessarily influenced by human passions born of the war. That spirit was incompatible with the ideals of a family of nations subject to international law. For that reason it can be said with justice that the League was organized as an alliance of governments more than as a democratic association to preserve international peace and the collective security of nations.

The League of Nations was the generous work of idealists, but it was doomed to failure because of the treaty which was the work of politicians. Universal public opinion did not have the opportunity to intervene in the elaboration and discussion of the Covenant of the League. An international accord of such a nature must be the work of democracy, that is to say, the voice of the people and the expression of a universal conscience, lightened by free discussion and the analysis of facts. Today it is evident that the League of Nations has been impotent in guaranteeing the main purpose of its existence: "to promote international co-operation and to achieve international peace and security." The renunciation of war, the maintenance of the integrity and the independence of states, the establishment of a régime of economic liberty and commercial freedom among nations and monetary stabilization have failed. Customs barriers have hindered the normal functioning of world commerce, and monetary disorder has rendered difficult freedom in the field of investments and credits.

Does this mean that the Covenant of the League does not work or that the establishment of a Society of Nations subject to international law is an impossible or unattainable dream? I think not.

I had the opportunity to witness at Geneva the hard test of the integral application of the Covenant in its most difficult hour during the autumn of 1935. In spite of the difficulties of procedure, Articles of the Covenant were, theoretically, executory. Notwithstanding the fact that the measures taken to stop aggression were lacking the essential conditions of functioning automatically and universally, the application of Article 16 did not present any juridical or constitutional obstacle. But the political execution of sanctions made evident the necessity of organizing the League of Nations upon a continental or regional basis. Particularly in the case of the American countries, intervention in matters exclusively European has at times been irritating, both to us and to the

European people. A universal federation integrated by regional or continental confederacies would make more feasible the achievement of the ideals which today are darkened by war. In the organization of peace, public opinion will have an important participation, not only in the belligerent countries but also in the neutral ones. The reappearance of the hopes fostered in 1919 shall be so strong that it will influence decisively the mind of the statesmen in charge of interpreting the will of the people. The best work of the sincere pacifist rests in keeping alert the intelligence of the people to intervene with all the weight of their will power in the creation of a new order and of a régime of relations among the nations regulated by international law. In this respect, the movement of public opinion to which Doctor Nicholas Murray Butler lends stimulus with his noble authority and his moral prestige is one of the best contributions to the reappearance of the ideals of liberty and respect for law, which are the foundation of the destiny of the Americas.

ANNOUNCER: We return you to New York—

DOCTOR BUTLER: I have the honor to present as next speaker the Chinese Ambassador to this country, Doctor Hu Shih, philosopher, man of letters, statesman. Again we take you to Washington—

DOCTOR HU SHIH: To all lovers of peace and international order, the twenty-first anniversary of Armistice Day must be a sad occasion indeed. A great war has been going on in East Asia for twenty-eight months; a greater war has been developing in Europe for seventy days, while the League of Nations—the great symbol of the post-war world order—has practically ceased to function. The dreams of the years of Wilsonian idealism seem now to have been completely shattered.

However, it profits us little to lament the failures and errors of the past. The bygone is beyond recall.

It may be more useful for us to reflect on the lessons which we should learn from these past failures so that the dreamers and builders of a future world order may be benefited by them.

In a remarkable address of two weeks ago, the new British Ambassador to the United States, the Marquess of Lothian, said:

One of the mistakes the democracies made after the last war was to think that peace would come in the main through disarmament. Disarmament on a large scale, of course, is necessary. But peace comes from there being overwhelming power behind law—as you found when you had to deal with the gangsters within your boundaries.

I think Lord Lothian has drawn the most important lesson that can be drawn from the recent history of international relationship and government. The future League or Union of Nations must be a "League to *Enforce* Peace." An international government that can not enforce its law and order is illusory and unreal.

In order to make this fundamental idea workable, a few guiding principles seem to be quite necessary:

First, the future world order must be built up on the basis, not of vague generalities and abstractions, but of definite and precise commitments by the states. The

Pact of Paris is an example of vague generalization. The British and French pledges to Poland, Rumania and Greece in 1939, on the other hand, are definite commitments. The Earl of Lytton once said: "It is broadly true, however paradoxical it may sound, that the greater and the more precise are the commitments of a country, the less is its liability to be drawn into war." Lord Lytton cited the Monroe Doctrine as a case of a definite commitment.

Second, the old idea of formal equality among the nations must be greatly qualified and supplemented by the principle of graded responsibility according to the ability, strength, and geographical or strategic position of the states. It is absurd, for instance, to expect Denmark to undertake the same responsibility as Great Britain in a given international situation. Why not therefore frankly recognize the fact and apportion the responsibilities according to their respective abilities?

Third, a necessary corollary from the idea of graded responsibility is the principle of regional leadership and co-operation. The fatal mistake of the League of Nations is that it could not effectively function even as a League of Europe. Its pretensions as a world government were largely responsible for the failure to set up regional machineries to deal effectively with important local conflicts. The historic part played by the United States in the Western Hemisphere best illustrates what I mean by the idea of regional leadership and co-operation. The future world government should be a super-federation of some such regional set-ups as the League of Europe, the Conference of American States, the British Commonwealth, the Conference of Pacific States, the Conference of Western and Southwestern Asiatic States, etc.

A world state of regional federations and confederacies with definite and precise commitments according to the graded responsibilities of the states or groups of states—this is the formula which I wish to recommend to the serious reflection of all dreamers of a better and more workable world order.

ANNOUNCER: We return you to New York—

DOCTOR BUTLER: I next have the honor to present Doctor Antonio Sánchez de Bustamante y Sirvén, distinguished jurist, who was a Delegate to the Second Peace Conference at The Hague in 1907 and to the Peace Conference in Paris in 1919. He has been a Member of the Permanent Court of Arbitration for over thirty years and Judge of the Permanent Court of International Justice since 1921. We take you now to Habana—

JUDGE DE BUSTAMANTE: Three great writers of ancient Rome have left us three well-known and popular sayings. In one of them, if it be interpreted with absolute exactness, might be found the fundamental reason for war. In the other two we find its condemnation and the grounds on which pacifism rests its case.

The first of these ancient sayings to which we refer is from Plautus, and it reads thus: "Homo homini lupus" —"Man is for man a wolf."

For the second, we are indebted to one for whom we have the greatest respect and affection, for it places the condemnation of military strife within the human heart.

It is Horace who speaks of "Bella matribus detestata"—
"War which the mothers detest."

And the third saying is from Terence, establishing
that solidarity of the human race which force attacks
and destroys. He formulated it thus: "Homo sum;
humani nihil a me alienum puto"—"I am human and
nothing human is of indifference to me."

When we have to take sides between these two opposed
tendencies, the soul and the heart side with the latter.
According to Christian doctrine, one must love one's
neighbor as one's self, and certainly one who engages
in maiming and exterminating his neighbor by all the
military resources at his command, on the ground that
a state of war exists, does not love but hate. Unfortunately war—the same as crimes against individuals—
has existed from the time that different social groups
began to appear in the world, and perhaps all efforts
for a long period of time merely tended toward making
it less frequent, fitting the action to the word of a
famous philosopher according to whom perpetual peace
"may be approximated indefinitely," which is equivalent
to saying that while it always gets nearer it will never
be reached.

Certainly it is true of internal national life that, no
matter how greatly customs may improve and civilization advance, there is always crime, and there will
always be the need of penal laws; but it is hardly possible to imagine what would happen if social ethics were
not taught and such laws did not serve to anticipate and
prevent criminal acts in a multitude of cases. We should
profit from the lessons learned in our national life and
act accordingly in international life.

In the first place, it is necessary that in the grade schools, the high schools and the universities emphasis be placed by teachers and professors on the horrors and injustices of war. Instead of celebrating the conquering generals and unjustly attributing to them epochs in human progress, the searchlight of reality should be turned on the immorality and injustice of the majority of wars, and perhaps of the majority of victories also; on what statistics show regarding the dead and maimed and the destruction of life and culture; on what these struggles really represent from the viewpoint of universal morality; and on what it would mean to the world to have a relatively long period of peace in which the thunder of cannon would not be heard and in which there would be a notable reduction of implements of war and of soldiers.

When youth is educated and matures in such an atmosphere, the principles of international law will be happily applied and will result in an increase of cases —of which there are already examples—in which a form of judicial authority has decided which among the states is right and has added to the moral force available for peaceful settlements. Man lives on culture, by culture and for culture, and war lives on the destruction of whatever culture exists when it starts, and it retards the culture of the future.

While war constitutes a crime on the part of whoever starts it without right or reason, it is necessarily also a scourge for those attacked, and there is no more effective way of preventing or diminishing the first evil than, by teaching from the primary school upward, to create the hatred of force and injustice and the firm determination not to collaborate with them, even though it may be said and believed that they will result in a material advantage. This teaching must be impressed upon the adult in such a way that he may not forget it, and it should always be held up before him in hours of crisis by the press, a most powerful factor in the forming of opinion, by books, and by this new means of education and propaganda that is called the radio. Man is susceptible to any propaganda that leads him toward the good, and even if at the beginning the result does not appeal to those who are impatient, in the long run the effort will be astonishing in the result produced. And then neither the people's representatives nor the ruling class, according to the form of government, will be able to force the people into military camps, definitely opposed to right and justice and, frequently, to civilization itself. To educate intensively for peace and the predominance of right by presenting to the mind the numerous proofs that demonstrate its advantages, is, without doubt, the most necessary and the most productive of all campaigns for peace. And since of war it can be said that it is always Hell, of peace it may then be said it is Paradise.

ANNOUNCER: We return you to Columbia in New York—

DOCTOR BUTLER: And, finally, we shall have the honor of hearing a message prepared for us by the distinguished President of Panamá, Doctor Juan Demóstenes Arosemena, but which he himself is prevented from delivering by reason of grave illness, from which, we are happy to report, he is recovering. The message of President Arosemena will be read by Sr. Doctor D. Augusto S. Boyd, the Ambassador of Panamá to the United States, who speaks to˙ you from Washington—

DOCTOR BOYD: It is my special privilege to read the address of the President of Panamá, which is as follows:

[MESSAGE OF PRESIDENT AROSEMENA]

I have accepted with pleasure the invitation extended to me by the Carnegie Endowment for International Peace to take part in its annual radio program on Armistice Day, because I consider that no man of good will should deny his aid toward the high purposes of such a generous institution.

There is not, nor can there ever be, any voice lost in reminding the peoples of the world that they form part of one large human family, a very simple and at the same time a very great truth, the clear understanding of which could bring a final and harmonic solution to the old and anguishing human drama.

I am personally convinced that the Carnegie Endowment for International Peace has done well in choosing the topic "Family of Nations" in order to develop around it its Christian propaganda in favor of universal peace, even though many people might feel inclined to smile ironically at the mere idea of an association of the domestic institution of the family with the spectacle of hate, destruction and death at which humanity gazes in our days.

War has never been a phenomenon of popular origin; conflicts between peoples have never developed from the spontaneous will of the people; their process of development has always started from a directing entity, which may be an autocrat or a dynasty, a social class or a religious caste, a political party or an economic group, that in a given historical moment has begun to form public opinion in favor of war and can count on sufficient means to influence it.

The stronger the directing entity is and the more concentrated it holds such authority, the surer it will be to carry a nation to war, because it will then be easier for the directing entity to dominate the propaganda means which prepare for war, decide upon it and turn it loose.

Herein lies the reason for the importance of *democratic education* as the most effective mean of creating a pacific attitude among the peoples of the world. It should be a democratic education that would not limit itself to recognizing the superiority of said political system of government and content itself with its more or less theoretical establishment, but appreciates that it signifies the true capacity of the masses to exercise themselves in the performance of their functions and rights in the accomplishment of civil duties.

It should be a democratic education capable of creating a deep sense of responsibility among those who govern and a vigilant and collective attitude among the masses capable of demanding it with energy. Such democratic education should extend beyond political boundaries the validity of international law as the only source of well-being and as the only guarantee of order, as well as the surest pledge of the stability, permanence and cordiality of mutual relations.

When the peoples of the earth think in the above-mentioned manner, then the apocalyptical monster of war will have received the most severe and effective blow, the monster which has never done any moral, material or intellectual benefit to any nation; and it is then that we shall properly be able to speak of the "Family of Nations."

ANNOUNCER: We take you back to Doctor Butler in New York—

DOCTOR BUTLER: The eloquent addresses from these outstanding scholars and statesmen to which we have just listened are abundant in wisdom. They should make it plain to us that the passions and ambitions which were set loose by the Great War have been operating, and still operate, to do the principles of democracy great damage and to shatter the foundations upon which any movement for international co-operation must be based.

XXVIII

BENEATH THE SURFACE

From the *Report of the President of Columbia University for 1939*

BENEATH THE SURFACE

The world of today is overcrowded wth information. The astonishing excellence of contemporary journalism and the rapidly growing service of the radio leave few happenings, whether important or unimportant, that are not brought to the attention of the whole world. Information, however, is not knowledge. Knowledge involves and implies an understanding of what information means, of how much of this information has lasting significance and of how its particulars are to be welded together to make possible a true comprehension of what this vast amount of information really signifies. The one instrument which makes possible the turning of information into knowledge is the philosophy of history. Indeed, the philosophy of history is the common denominator of every numerator which enters into the intellectual life or the educational process. It is only through and by the philosophy of history that the story of humanity may be told and understood. It is, therefore, the one wholly essential subject of lifelong study on the part of intelligent human beings. The world has had for more than a century and a half an example of what the philosophy of history means and what the philosophy of history may teach. That example is provided by Edward Gibbon's *History of the Decline and Fall of the Roman Empire,* than which perhaps no greater book has ever been written. On its pages is told the story of the greatest of world political organizations at the height of its significance and power. Then there follows on those same pages that superbly told story of how that great empire came to its end and was laid in ashes.

All change in the history of civilization has taken place in one of two ways. Usually it has taken place slowly and gradually through the process of evolution. New and sometimes invisible forces are at work, now here and now there, shaping and reshaping men's mode of thought, changing their relation to environment and leading or guiding them to a change or reorganization of their social, economic and political institutions. Or these changes may take place, as they have done more than once, by the violent process of revolution. In such case, what the student of the philosophy of history sees is the storing up behind some barrier of a new and powerful force, usually emotional in character and in expression, which suddenly and with terrifying accompaniments breaks down the barriers which hold it in check and destroys in a few short years all that has been accomplished through centuries and starts mankind on a new and wholly different path. If American independence was gained by evolution extending over some two hundred years in the history of the English people, the French Revolution was truly revolutionary both in form and in its results, including the years of Napoleonic domination.

What sort of change is it through which the world is passing today? Is the force behind that change evolution or revolution? No more vitally important question is to be pressed at this moment upon the attention not only of university scholars and their students, but upon the public opinion of the world. Fortunately, there have been published in recent years four outstanding contributions to the philosophy of history, and to them one may turn for most helpful guidance in trying to reach an understanding of what is really going on in this twentieth-century world. One of these works is from England, one is from Italy, one is from Spain and one is from Germany.

The English work is *A History of Europe,* by Herbert A. L. Fisher, the distinguished Warden of New College, Oxford.[1] This work is already recognized as a classic and will take its place by the side of Gibbon's *History of the Decline and Fall of the Roman Empire.* The third volume of the original edition of this work is entitled *History of the Liberal Movement,* and the last chapter of that volume is called "The Old Democracies and the New Dictators." Here is the point at which to begin to read this truly great work at the present time.

The second book is by the distinguished Italian philosopher and political scientist, Signor Gaetano Mosca, and is entitled *The Ruling Class.*[2] This work, which is now some thirty years old, has been known to scholars in Italy and in France for a generation, but only during the past year has it appeared in English translation, with a most illuminating introduction by Professor Arthur Livingston of the Department of Romance Languages of Columbia University. Signor Mosca has drawn a most convincing picture of the way in which, through times that are past, different groups, tendencies,

---

[1]Fisher, Herbert A. L., *A History of Europe* (London: Eyre and Spottiswoode, 1935). 3 vols. This work is now available in one volume.

[2]Mosca, Gaetano, *The Ruling Class* (New York: McGraw-Hill Book Company, 1939).

interests and ambitions have succeeded each other in the exercise of power over their fellow men and over economic and political institutions.

The third book is by the Spanish scholar, Señor Ortega y Gasset, and is called *The Revolt of the Masses*.[3] Ortega y Gasset offers another, and in a sense parallel, analysis of the forces which in time past have marked the rise and fall of change in western civilization.

Finally, the fourth book is the much-discussed *Decline of the West*, by the German, Oswald Spengler.[4] Spengler's book was written before the outbreak of the Great War of 1914–18 and was first published in Germany just as that war was coming to its end. It was received in countries other than Germany with interest tempered by sarcasm. As the years have passed, the interest has tended to increase and the sarcasm has shown signs of diminishing. Whatever may be thought of Spengler's argument, his book must be read, and read in connection with the works of Fisher, Mosca and Ortega, if one is to approach the underlying problems of today with open mind and willingness to face the distasteful. Such democracies as are left in the world are finding their obligations to their fellow men increased in geometrical progression as the democracies themselves diminish in number or become subject to disintegrating forces within their own boundaries.

The first and most convincing lesson which the twentieth-century student of the philosophy of history will

[3]Ortega y Gasset, José, *The Revolt of the Masses* (New York: W. W. Norton and Company, 1932).

[4]Spengler, Oswald, *The Decline of the West* (New York: Alfred A. Knopf, 1934).

learn is that the world of today is essentially a unit, and that continents, national boundaries, languages and alleged differences of race as obstacles to human co-operation toward the highest human ends are all terms which belong to centuries now past. Any and every force set loose in the world exerts influence over the whole world. The political and economic isolation which is still taught by the intellectually halt, maimed and blind has, and can have, no existence under present-day conditions. The task before the world of today is to gain what information can be had from every possible source and then to go beneath that information to those wellsprings of knowledge and of understanding which will enable us to know what that information really means and reveals.

XXIX

NEW YEAR MESSAGE, 1940

A public statement published on
New Year's Day, 1940

NEW YEAR MESSAGE, 1940

As the year 1939 ends, with its appalling record of moral, economic and political disaster, it takes some courage to look forward with hope. Yet that courage is demanded by every interest of the American people and of the civilized world. The foundations of that world are shaking. What causes that shaking is the rapidly growing strength of those highly reactionary social and economic doctrines and policies which, having been preached throughout the western world for a century, seemed harmless enough so long as they were confined to words. When, however, they are transformed into deeds through acts of despotism, of shocking immorality and of lawlessness on a huge scale, they can no longer be treated with unconcern. Not only is there now challenge to every fundamental doctrine of that philosophy of Liberalism which had been steadily extending its influence over Europe and the Americas for fully four hundred years, but Liberalism itself is sneered at and treated with contempt. The philosophy of Power is in the saddle. That philosophy manifests itself in action by the use of force. As between organized nations, this force is at first economic and then military. Within the boundaries of a given nation, the manifestations of this force are at first economic and then political. In either case, the foundations of democracy are undermined, whether upon that democracy as a foundation be built a republic or a monarchy. We are now back again in an era when

certain peoples or groups regard themselves as having
been selected by an Almighty God whose existence they
deny and whose name they flaunt, to rule not only their
quiet and unoffending neighbors but the whole world.
In other words, our civilization has been put back to the
point where the ancient Roman civilization was when it
was challenged and attacked by Alaric the Goth and
Attila the Hun. We have our twentieth-century Alaric
and our twentieth-century Attila.

In the face of this most disturbing and frightening
situation, a stupendous amount of nonsense is being
spoken and written. We in the United States are assured
that all these happenings are no concern of ours but
that we are remote and aloof from the unfortunate
world in which they are taking place. We are assured
that we must turn attention, not alone first but only, to
our own domestic concerns and let the other peoples on
this earth look out for themselves. Could there be
more fantastic nonsense than this? It comes from the
lips and the pens of those who day by day and hour by
hour turn on the radio and listen to what is being said
and done in Great Britain and in France, in Germany
and in Russia, in Italy and in the Balkans, in Japan and
in Argentina. It comes from the lips and pens of those
who see our American economic depression of a decade
stoutly resisting all efforts at Washington and the state
capitals to relieve it, for the simple reason that it is
part of a world depression and of a world economic
crisis which cannot be dealt with or relieved except on
a world-wide basis and by world-wide policies.

If the American people propose to save their own
fundamental institutions and to protect the foundations

upon which those institutions rest, they must without delay put a stop to the rule of force as a substitute for the rule of reason in dealing with their own economic and social problems. They must grasp leadership in a world-wide movement for world-wide co-operation, first, to resist the overturn of Liberalism by force and, second, to build a new world-wide organization on the principles of Liberalism as these have been exemplified and illustrated in the government and political history of the American people.

It must not be forgotten that the aggressors are not waging declared wars. All those huge military and naval operations of which we read hour by hour are not part of any declared war by the aggressor nations. They simply seized upon these methods of terrorizing and assuming control over neighbor nations which happen to be smaller in area, of less population and therefore less powerful than themselves. The obvious and privately declared aim of those who for the moment control the once great German people is to take over, without declared war, the Scandinavian countries, the Netherlands and Belgium, so as to control the seas to the west. It is similarly their privately declared purpose to take over Hungary and, if relations with Russia make it possible, Rumania, and thereby open the way to control of the Black Sea and the Dardanelles. When this has been done, they propose to say to Great Britain and to France: "You are now in the same position as Portugal. That country, too, had world-wide colonies and sea control once upon a time, but it has these no longer. Stay out there on the Atlantic, like Portugal. Go west as much as you like, but we propose to control everything east of the Strait of Dover and the Rhine. France and Italy may arrange for the control of the Mediterranean and North Africa as they think best." There has been no secret about this ambition for some time past, although it has not yet been flaunted before the public.

If the American people are really to deal with intelligence and success with what are called their own problems, they must no longer delay in accepting and vigorously acting upon the constructive economic and monetary policies unanimously adopted by the famous Conference held at Chatham House in March, 1935. They must proceed to take the lead in setting up that system of world organization by which alone these matters can be satisfactorily dealt with and the foundations laid for a world that can become prosperous and that can remain at peace. The challenge to the American people is imperative.

XXX
THE REAL ISSUE

An address delivered at the annual meeting
of The Pilgrims of the United States,
Hotel Biltmore, New York,
January 24, 1940

THE REAL ISSUE

My Fellow Pilgrims: The clouds which were hanging over the world at the time of our last annual meeting have grown vastly darker and more threatening during the year which has passed. They are the darkest and the most threatening clouds which have hung over this western world since the fall of the Roman Empire. This is due not only to the characteristics of those clouds themselves, but also and largely to the fact that the world of today is a very different one from what it ever has been before. Bound together by information and by contact, intellectual, economic, social, and political, by the electric spark, there is now no part of the settled world which is beyond the reach and outside of the influence of any important happening anywhere.

The extraordinary thing for those of us who are Pilgrims is that we must now find ourselves face to face with the fact that the fundamental principles to which we are devoted, the fundamental institutions which our English-speaking ancestors have been engaged in building for a thousand years, have not only ceased to have influence in new and distant lands, but are openly and vigorously challenged both within our own land and in other parts of the world where quite opposite theories and doctrines have established themselves.

What has become of the old, constructive, forward-facing, historic Liberalism which during the eighteenth and nineteenth centuries dominated the thought and the public life of the English-speaking peoples? Where are the voices that led us on? Where are the prophets, the Chathams, the Burkes, the Pitts, the Washingtons, the Hamiltons, the Jeffersons, the Madisons, to stand before the whole world to proclaim, defend and interpret those principles written into our Federal Constitution with its Bill of Rights, and accepted by the British people through custom and long habit, without being written into a specific constitutional document? What has become of them?

If we are to give an intelligent answer to that question, we must go back over just about one hundred years. You will then find coming into the life and thought of Europe a new doctrine, a doctrine at first preached by philosophers and theoretical intellectuals, and not accepted either quickly or by any considerable measure of men. But, as the years have passed, that new, that revolutionary doctrine has steadily grown in force and today is the open and declared enemy of our historic principles of liberty, political, social, economic, intellectual and religious.

What is that new principle? That principle, first taught by the German philosopher Hegel, is that the state must be antecedent to and superior to the individual citizen, and that the state has in itself the power, the authority and the right to turn the individual to such purposes by such methods and under such limitations as may seem to it desirable and wise. But how could there be a state before there were individuals? Surely the individuals constitute the state, and surely the state, as the philosophers define it and use the term, must therefore be a purely theoretical, abstract word to indicate their principle and their point of view.

At first that doctrine was discussed abstractly only and in a general way; but pretty soon, and largely by the skill and persistence of Karl Marx and those who were associated with him, it was translated into specific doctrines of antagonism and opposition to free institutions, resisting their approach to lands where they had not been established and attacking the foundations of free institutions in those lands which they controlled.

We have now been engaged, my fellow Pilgrims, in that struggle for the better part of a hundred years. It has taken on new and terrifying forms because, for psychological and historical reasons, with which you are all familiar, that doctrine has taken possession of populations of immense size, of great physical power and of enormous natural resources, and, where it has control, liberty will not be permitted to exist. It will not only disappear, but it will be wrecked and demolished if force can manage to do that.

Moreover, this doctrine was the first of all political doctrines openly to claim international influence and international control. Lovers of liberty in the English-speaking countries and in France, in the Scandinavian and Dutch countries and in Switzerland were all willing to practise liberty, to try to improve liberty, to try to show the value of liberty, and then to let it make its appeal to other nations in an educational fashion, bit by bit. That is where we were fifty years ago. We were at a point, following the war between Germany and France, where the doctrines of liberty seemed to be gaining ground here and there, except, of course, in the despotic monarchy which ruled the Russian people. At that time Italy, Germany, Austria, all seemed to be becoming open-minded and to accept in some degree these doctrines with which the English-speaking peoples have been associated since Magna Carta.

But now resistance to liberty has become so definite, so specific and so terrifying, that everything in which we believe, everything of the foundations upon which our institutions are built, is at stake in this world-wide war of so-called ideologies or ideas. The fighting troops are but a very small part of this contest. The real controversy is between two types of civilization, two types of life, two ideals of government and social order. That conflict, if settled against us, will put the world back for generations to come; if settled for us—and that is something to which we must devote our intelligence—we may be able to remove this huge obstacle to progress and to call back true Liberalism to its place of control in a progressive and a peaceful world. But, in order to do that, we must clearly understand the issue.

All of these attacks upon the philosophy of liberty are not made openly. They are often made quietly, almost surreptitiously, by taking down this barrier and that between liberty and state control. Now it is one particular object, due to the activity of a well-organized and self-seeking minority; now it is another and similar undertaking, using the first as a precedent. So, little by little, you find transformation going on, even in the liberty-loving countries, France, Great Britain and the United States, without any open confession of knowledge of the fact that a fundamental controversy is at work between two absolutely conflicting principles of life and of government.

What are we going to do about it? To answer that

question, just a word must be said about a new and rather interesting form of attack upon liberty which surrounds us on every side. We are now told that if you speak of this at a time when there is such difference of opinion in the world, you are engaged in propaganda, and that must not be permitted. What is propaganda? The word came into existence three hundred years ago when the Vatican established its *Congregatio de Propaganda Fide*, its Division for Propagating the Faith, the Christian Faith. It was the name of the missionary movement of the Christian Church throughout the world. Then it passed into meaning argument in favor of anything in which the speaker believed. Then it took on the form which is now attempted to be given to it—the heretical teaching of a false doctrine. The result is that the public mind is very greatly confused by the term. As a matter of fact, there is not a particle of difference between true propaganda and education. Education is propaganda. If you learn the multiplication table, it is propaganda that two and two do not make five; and it is very important that that fact should be grasped.

Now we are told that, if those of us who are believers in liberty and devoted to its support and continuance talk much of liberty at a time like this, we are engaging in propaganda. So be it! Any one who speaks English is called a propagandist. I have been engaged in propaganda all my life in favor of the underlying American principles of government, trying to show other peoples their significance, their value, their importance and their success, and I have not the slightest intention of being diverted from propaganda because such work is called by that name.

One word more: We must realize the fact that in the doctrine called Socialism, there are ends in view which are wholly admirable—care of one's fellows, devotion to the common and general interest, solicitude for the less fortunate members of the human family. These are excellent, every one of them. The difficulty is that the methods proposed by Socialists to achieve those ends are wrong and unnecessary. They can all be achieved through the doctrines of liberty on two conditions: first, that those doctrines be taught and practised with intelligence and on the ground of moral principle; and second, that the gain-seeking instinct, the mean desire to trade upon and to make use of one's fellow man, be excluded from individual life and from public policy. These admirable ends may then be achieved, as they all can be, in terms of the fundamental doctrines of Anglo-Saxon liberty.

My friends, it is of vital importance that we reflect upon this world situation and that we realize that the doctrine of the superiority of the state, now armed with a strength which no such doctrine has ever had before, is fully conscious of what it is trying to do. It has no notion of contenting itself with meeting the present, the immediate political ambitions of the governments which it dominates. Its intention, often expressed in private, and soon to be told in public, is to wage war on the fundamental doctrines of civil, political, religious and economic liberty, until the whole world has been reduced to state-controlled compulsion. That is the alternative which faces America, Great Britain, and the world, as we enter upon a new decade.

INDEX

Acropolis, 159 ff.; 241 f.
Adams, John, 59, 110
Agence Litteraire Internationale, Paris, article written for, July 21, 1938, 71–74
Agriculture, labor problem created by introduction of machinery, 174
Aix-la-Chapelle, 160
Alaric, 304
Alexander the Great, 15, 168
Ambassador, service of, 248 ff.
America, North, and South, Aranha on co-operation in, 278 ff.
American Club in Paris, The, address, June 14, 1938, 57–68
American college, and education for peace, 153 ff.; peculiarly American, 153; development, 153 f.; different from Gymnasium and Lycée, 154
American literature, 214 f.; little known in England, 187 f.
Antonines, Gibbon on, 249 f.
Aranha, Oswaldo, address, 276–80
Argonaut, The, article written for, 35–37
Aristotle, on Ochlocracy, 196
Armaments, limitation of, 24, 61, 63
Armistice Day, broadcasts (1938), 121–43; (1939), 273–92
Arosemena, Juan Demóstenes, address, 289–92
Association of Urban Universities, address, October 24, 1939, 239–44
Athens, as world capital, 159 ff.
Attila, 304

Babel, Tower of, source of world problems, 35 f., 168
Bacon, Roger, 41
Bankers Club, New York, address, January 25, 1939, 159–63

Barbarism, return to, 80 f.
Belgium, 266
Bell, Alexander Graham, 41
Bill of Rights, U. S., 110, 162 f., 228; importance of, 179; four freedoms assured by, 183–84
Bismarck, Prince, 72; "Dropping the Pilot," 151–52
Borah, William E., speech on the Neutrality Act, 227
Boyd, Augusto S., 290
Briand, Aristide, 64, 73; Pact of Paris, 262
British Commonwealth of Nations, 72, 148; Act of 1931, 178
Bryce, James, 247
Bureaucracy, threat to Democracy, 93
Burke, Edmund, on duty to his constituents, 90; publication of complete works, 188
Business, 43–44
Bustamente y Sirvén, Antonio Sánchez de, address, 286–89
Butler, Nicholas Murray, sent to Europe by Taft, 113; cited by Henry-Haye on peace based on reality, 130; Aranha on influence of, 276; Turbay on influence of, 283

Cambridge University, 153
Canada, Chatham House Conference, 266
Canberra, Australia, 162
Capitalism, and capital, defined, 83, 215 f.
Carnegie Endowment for International Peace, 65, 276 f., 290; *International Conciliation*, 264
Cercle Interallié, address, June 14, 1938, 57–68

315